DIEN BIEN PHU

Dien Bien Phu Valley,
viewed from the high
ground in early 1954.

BATTLES IN FOCUS

# DIEN BIEN PHU

DAVID STONE

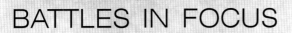

BRASSEY'S

First published in 2004 by Brassey's

An imprint of Chrysalis Books Group plc

Brassey's
The Chrysalis Building, Bramley Road,
London W10 6SP
www.chrysalisbooks.co.uk

Distributed in North America by:
Casemate Publishing, 2114 Darby Road,
Havertown, PA 19083, USA

David Stone has asserted his moral right
to be identified as the author of this work.

Library of Congress Cataloging in Publication Data
available

British Library Cataloguing-in-Publication Data:
a catalogue record for this book is available
from the British Library

ISBN 1 85753 372 0

Photograph acknowledgements: pages 28, 56, 70,
ECPAD France; pages 40, 67, 86–87, 104, SIRPA;
pages 90–91, 94, Photo Rondy; other illustrations
Chrysalis Images.

Edited and designed by DAG Publications Ltd
Designed by David Gibbons
Edited by Michael Boxall
Cartography and layout by Anthony A. Evans

Printed in Singapore

# CONTENTS

# AUTHOR'S NOTE

A number of accounts – both in French and in English – of the Battle of Dien Bien Phu are available today. Some of these deal with specific aspects of the battle in considerable detail, others with the battle in its entirety.[1] Several mention the battle incidentally, within wider histories of the French army units involved – especially those of the French Foreign Legion or the French paratroops. Dien Bien Phu has also featured at various levels of detail in a number of general books on post-1945 military history. In addition, the many lessons of this battle have been analysed in the military staff training publications of several armies. Despite the existence of such a wealth of information, in the course of researching this book it became increasingly clear that there were in some cases factual discrepancies between these often diverse accounts – particularly where weapon and equipment holdings, force levels and organisations, and statistical summaries were concerned; but also between their differing descriptions of the actions of some individuals and units (especially below battalion-level).

Consequently, in this account of the Battle of Dien Bien Phu, the subject has been approached in two ways. First, apart from a few essential exceptions, it concentrates on the French Union side of the conflict at battalion-level or above, and on the communist Viet Minh (or the 'People's Army of Vietnam') forces generally at army and division-level. Second, this work attempts – through research and (in a very few cases) the application of a measure of professional military judgement – to rationalise and resolve the more important factual inconsistencies identified in some other accounts. Therefore, it is postulated that the resultant work is an accurate and authoritative account of all the key elements of the battle of Dien Bien Phu, together with a new perspective on many of the events and decisions that surrounded and influenced the course of this remarkable clash of arms – a defining moment in French and Vietnamese history, and unquestionably one of the most important battles of the Cold War era.

Finally, my particular thanks to Colonel (Retired) Nigel Flower, a long-term friend and a former colleague in the world of military intelligence. The final text of this work has benefited enormously from his positive suggestions and critical comments; but especially from the uniquely authoritative nature of these, consequent upon his special knowledge of Indo-China due to his assignment in former times as the UK Military Attaché in Vientiane, Laos, at the height of America's war in Vietnam.

# INTRODUCTION

In mid-1966, I was serving on a short attachment to the 11e Bataillon de Chasseurs Alpins (the French Army's light infantry mountain warfare specialists). The battalion was stationed in the sleepy little town of Barcelonette in the Bas-Alpes. En route to Barcelonette I had spent a few days in the capital, where Paris was still showing signs of the earlier turmoil that had engulfed part of the French army. Only five years before, following what many viewed as the betrayal of the French army by General de Gaulle and the Paris government over its abandonment of Algeria, elements of the French Foreign Legion had mutinied, together with some other élite units and individuals. The Legion's principal combat unit – the 1er Régiment Étranger de Parachutistes (1 REP) – had been disbanded, and the political reliability of a large element in the Legion and paratroop regiments remained uncertain in the eyes of the government. Elsewhere, strong undercurrents of political and national uncertainty persisted. Indeed, in 1966, in a mood of continuing paranoia in metropolitan France, several public buildings in Paris retained the rooftop machine-gun positions set up some five or six years earlier to counter an anticipated coup. But in Barcelonette such heady matters seemed far removed from the daily life of the Chasseurs Alpins in the picturesque French alpine region.

Then, one evening in the *sous-officiers'* mess I encountered an *adjudant-chef* (senior warrant officer) whose three or four rows of medal ribbons, together with the paratrooper's qualification wings on his chest and the green and gold '*fourragère*' of the Médaille Militaire at his shoulder, indicated the extent of this man's service. As the sun dropped below the mountains and the shadows lengthened outside, we talked. It transpired that he was completing the final months of his military service in the region in which he intended to settle as a civilian, and was happy to recount something of his military service to a ready listener from England. He told of his time in Indo-China and in Algeria. He spoke about a great battle that had taken place in a wide and fertile valley in north-west Tonkin close to the border with Laos; a major – but fatally flawed – military operation that had been designed finally to defeat the communist Viet Minh in northern Indo-China. He recalled the fate of many of his comrades for whom that battle had been their last; and he was still in no doubt that the responsibility for their deaths on that particular battlefield lay squarely at the door of the French politicians of the day. But then, as he observed, throughout history the French army had always been betrayed by the politicians in Paris, and occasionally by its generals as well; it was ever thus, and this was the burden that a French soldier must accept as an unavoidable consequence of his duty. Outside, the summer evening had long ago become night. He talked on. As he did so, the political tensions that I had noted in Paris came ever more into perspective, as I began to understand something of the impact of the wars in Indo-China, and Algeria upon the very soul of France and its army.

When I finally bade my new-found acquaintance and raconteur goodnight the mess was almost deserted; while the small collection of empty Kronenbourg bottles on our table and the clock behind the bar bore testimony to the several hours that we had talked. As I walked to my accommodation, his tales of soldiering in Cochin-China, Annam and Tonkin – of that final cataclysmic struggle close to the Laotian border in 1954 in particular – remained vividly in my mind. By the time that I arrived at my quarters, I was sure that I would one day write an account of France's war in Indo-China: specifically about the dramatic events, the heroism, the pathos and the enormous historical and military impact of the final great armed conflict of that war – the battle of Dien Bien Phu.

Below: General Navarre (left), the French Union Forces Commander-in-Chief in Indo-China, in 1953.

# PREFACE

The battle that took place in the valley of Dien Bien Phu – literally the 'administrative centre of the border region' close to the Laotian border – to the west of Tonkin province was one of the most important clashes of arms of the twentieth century, and it could be argued that it was the most important battle involving a European power in the post-1945 period. For France, it was every bit as significant as the defeat that the imperial army of Napoleon III had suffered at the hands of Germany at Sedan almost a century before, in 1870: a military débâcle that in some respects echoed aspects of the conflict at Dien Bien Phu. At Sedan the French Army of Châlons was confined in a valley strong-point by the German forces, all the surrounding hills being occupied by the technologically superior German artillery which was able to observe and bring down an incessant and withering fire upon the immobile French forces. Even the immediate aftermath of Sedan, with a mass surrender of the French forces, inadequate arrangements for the prisoners taken, and their removal into the hinterland of their enemies resembled (albeit superficially) the events that followed Dien Bien Phu. Meanwhile, at the strategic and international level, Sedan signalled the end of the Napoléonic dynasty and the French Second Empire, and the birth of the German empire; just as Dien Bien Phu precipitated the end of France's colonial empire, the rise and return to power of General de Gaulle, and the creation of the sovereign states of North and South Vietnam. This in turn led to a further twenty years of warfare in Indo-China, and eventually culminated in the defeat of yet another great power at the hands of the North Vietnamese communists – but this time the vanquished would be no lesser nation than the United States of America.

The huge importance of Dien Bien Phu for France and its army was almost incalculable. Quite apart from the many essentially military lessons learnt, from that single great battle in Tonkin flowed years of political turmoil in a country and nation still trying to come to terms with the ignominious defeat of 1940, with the subsequent years of German occupation, with the years of the Vichy régime, and with the eventual liberation by the Western Allies. Despite Marshall Aid,[2] the French people were also still coping with the legacy of collateral damage and civilian casualties that liberation had inevitably inflicted upon much of northern France. But Dien Bien Phu was also the catalyst for change that further widened what was already an almost unbridgeable gap between the French government and a significant part of the regular French army: many of whose units and organisations had been fighting and dying on the front lines of France's colonial wars since 1945.

One organisation in particular was changed forever by Dien Bien Phu: the French Foreign Legion, which had been fighting for France in North Africa, and in some of the most inhospitable, disease-ridden and far-flung French colonies and territories ever since 1831. At Dien Bien Phu the Legion amassed further glory, but it was also politicised by a conflict in Indo-China that had so clearly been mismanaged by an uncaring and inept government in Paris and an apathetic or openly hostile population in metropolitan France. For the élite regular units of a justifiably proud but (in the view of many professional officers and soldiers) now betrayed French army, the seeds of disillusion and unease sown during almost ten years battling the Viet Minh finally germinated at Dien Bien Phu. They then blossomed and burst forth during the subsequent conflict in French Algeria; culminating in mutiny, criminality and terrorism – with the consequent dishonour and punishment of numerous senior officers, junior officers and soldiers, and the disgrace of a number of justifiably once-proud units. For the French Foreign Legion, the final abandonment of Algeria in 1962 was both an annulment of the unwritten contract between the Legion and France, and the abrogation of the Legion's very *raison d'être*.

Thus Dien Bien Phu and its aftermath exposed the nadir of French global military power in a long process of decline that had in reality begun more than one and a half centuries earlier, at the hands of the British and Prussians on the battlefield of Waterloo. For the French army, after Indo-China and Algeria nothing could ever be the same again, and for the Legion and the regular army alike these conflicts served to provide a new beginning, and allowed France, quite correctly, to develop its armed forces in a European and (albeit qualified) NATO context rather than as the imperialistic and colonising forces they had been for some three or four centuries. Although traumatic, the change has been good for the army, and its uniquely French approach to intervention overseas, co-operation, multi-nationalism, and the avoidance of the post-1990 political correctness[3] that has increasingly be-devilled and weakened many other western European armies since the end of the Cold War, has ensured that France now has forces of which it can again be proud, and which are well up to dealing with modern military missions internally and externally in a troubled and unstable world. And Dien Bien Phu and its aftermath were, indirectly, major contributors to this process of change.

One potential consequence of Dien Bien Phu was particularly dramatic, for at one stage the battle might well have become the scene of the first use of atomic weapons by the United States since Hiroshima and Nagasaki, in order to retrieve the otherwise hopeless French military situation. Had this attack been carried out, the escalation of the conflict beyond the region would have been virtually inevitable. In 1954 it was some five years since the Soviet Union had carried out its own first successful atomic explosion, and so the potential global implications of the US use of atomic weapons in Indo-China were all too obvious. Nevertheless, the US plan had been made, suitably small yield atomic weapons identified for the task, and presidential authority would probably have been forthcoming to strike the Viet Minh positions around the Dien Bien Phu valley with air-dropped atomic bombs. However, the British Prime Minister Winston

Churchill refused to authorise the wholehearted military involvement of Great Britain in the Indo-China venture, and this was a non-negotiable pre-condition for US action that had been set by the US Congress, together with France being required to abandon its future claims to its Far East territories – a requirement to which Paris was in any case not prepared to accede. Consequently, neither atomic nor conventional bombing by the USAF were forthcoming to save the beleaguered garrison, and this contributed directly to the often difficult state of US-Anglo-French relations during the 1950s and 1960s. It also confirmed de Gaulle's views and prejudices concerning the motives of his erstwhile Second World War allies, the position of France in NATO, and the urgent need for France to forgo its defence reliance on the United States and to develop its own independent strategic nuclear capability. Later, US intervention to foreclose the Anglo-French Suez operation in 1956 served to confirm and finally set the seal on de Gaulle's view of the administration in Washington.

But if the impact of Dien Bien Phu for France was enormous, its wider international consequences were just as significant. The French defeat might indeed have ended the First Indo-China War 1945–54, but in practice it directly paved the way for the Second Indo-China War – the Vietnam War – and for the escalating US involvement in the region. At the same time, the military defeat of a major European power by what was viewed as a communist insurgent army confirmed the post-1945 vulnerability of the European powers, and the perception in many parts of the world that the day of their once-great empires was indeed past. Clearly, the red star of communism was in the ascendancy, and such perceptions fuelled the many existing and embryo communist and nationalist movements in the remaining European colonies in the Far East, Asia and Africa; and also bolstered the Soviet Union's stranglehold on eastern Europe.

Thus the battle of Dien Bien Phu was indeed a defining moment in the history of warfare, that of the world in general and of the Cold War in particular.

# 1

# THE CONFLICT IN FRENCH INDO-CHINA

The long, bitter struggle of the peoples of French Indo-China and (since 1954) of Vietnam, Laos and Cambodia, to shape their future has been extensively documented and much studied during the last half century. The war carried on by the communists against the French from 1946 to 1954 is often dealt with as a separate conflict from that which took place from 1954 against the South Vietnamese government and, soon thereafter, against the United States and its allies. However, a constant thread that ran from 1946 through to 1975 was the nature and motivation of the indigenous communist enemy and its political and military leaders. The movement began fairly inauspiciously with the founding of a Communist Party of Indo-China in 1930. From the 1940s, however, Ho Chi Minh and his military commander Vo Nguyen Giap transformed the old states and kingdoms of Indo-China – Cochin China, Tonkin, Annam (which together comprised Vietnam), Cambodia and Laos – from their 1893 status as part of the French colonial empire, into three communist-dominated sovereign states in 1975.

Throughout, this epic struggle was fought in the jungles, plains and mountains of Vietnam, and in the villages and cities of a country and region that became a perpetual battleground for three decades. Vietnam's several mighty rivers, few all-weather road routes and countless jungle trails were the vital arteries along which flowed the armies and the *matériel* support that sustained them. Indeed, in terms of actual combat, a great deal of the Cold War that began in 1945 was in fact fought in South-East Asia: in French Indo-China, in the Republic of Korea, in Malaya and in the Republic of South Vietnam. And all of these conflicts were to varying degrees instrumental in shaping the fortunes and future strategic policies of Great Britain, France and the United States of America; the latter two countries in particular.

After 1945 Great Britain's pragmatic policies for the transformation of its empire into the British Commonwealth pre-empted the usual arguments advanced by nationalist and liberation movements in many other European protectorates and colonies. Malaya was a prime example of this. Similarly, the view of communism that prevailed in Great Britain throughout the immediate post-Second World War years was much less ideological than that in the United States, where anti-communism was already rapidly assuming the status of a crusade.

But the French view of its overseas territories was somewhat different from that held by the British. Many of its possessions, in Indo-China especially, were relatively recent acquisitions – gained between 1862 and 1893 – and France derived many economic, trade and strategic benefits from them; just as many individual diplomatic, military and civil service careers benefited enormously from service in French Indo-China. Also, over a hundred-year period, much blood had been shed by the military forces of France (by the French Foreign Legion in particular) to secure its possessions in South-East Asia and North Africa. Meanwhile, in the liberated Paris of 1945 there was a popular if somewhat misplaced perception that France was once again a great power, and that the pre-1940 world would now be restored. Therefore, the French government was not minded to give up to any indigenous administration – communist or nationalist – the French territory in Indo-China that had been temporarily stolen by the Japanese in 1941. The decision that followed, to maintain total control of French Indo-China, eventually resulted in some 81,760 dead servicemen, including 11,620 legionnaires and 26,686 Indo-Chinese soldiers (mainly of the Vietnamese national army). It also indirectly paved the way for France's subsequent defeat in Algeria, and the crisis that overtook the French army in 1961.

Apart from signalling the end of France as a great military and imperial power, the great significance of the events that took place in Indo-China from 1945 to 1954 was the way in which, imperceptibly at first and then with increasing inevitability, Vietnam changed from a French colonial battlefield to one on which the United States subsequently chose to make its stand against what the US commander in Korea in 1951, General Matthew B. Ridgway, called the 'dead existence of a Godless world' and the 'misery and despair' of communism. Arguably, the long-term scar that the US involvement left on America from 1975 was even greater than the crushing blow that France suffered in 1954. So how did this chain of events come about?

The military collapse at the hands of the Germans in 1940 provided a clear indication that France's fortunes were truly in decline, and this fact was lost neither upon the Japanese, who proceeded to seize the French, British and Dutch territories in the Far East from 1941, nor upon the several nationalist organisations within those territories who assessed that the time for action had at last arrived. In French Indo-China one such organisation was the League for the Independence of Vietnam ('Viet Nam Doc Lap Dong Minh Hoi', or 'Viet Minh'), headed by the communist Ho Chi Minh. He was a native of Annam, the narrow strip of territory which ran almost the full length of the country from Cochin China in the south to Tonkin (and the Chinese border) in the north and was the main province of Vietnam, bordering both Cambodia and Laos along most of its length. To the east of Annam lay the coast, and beyond it was the South China Sea.

Under the guidance of its military leader, Vo Nguyen Giap – a man whose early life had shaped and borne significantly upon his rise within the Indo-Chinese communist movement,[4] the Viet Minh carried out an effective guerrilla campaign against the French Vichy administration and Japanese occupation forces in the northern part of Indo-China, while co-ordinating its activities with other nationalist movements in the country. Indeed, the Viet Minh organisation was already expanding into main force, district guerrilla groups and village units, so that by early 1945 its development into a formidable armed force was progressing well.

In March 1945 the Japanese took savage military action against the small French garrisons (manned predominantly by legionnaires of the 5e Régiment Étranger d'Infanterie (5 REI) of the French Foreign Legion) that were scattered about the country. This act of treachery removed the token Vichy French administration headed by a number of pro-Japanese collaborators and enabled the Viet Minh to concentrate all its efforts against the Japanese. In turn, this produced increased military support from the United States, which now viewed the Viet Minh as the principal counter-Japanese force in the country. Apart from this, President Roosevelt had already made his position on Indo-China clear on 24 January 1944, when he indicated that France should vacate the country and permit the several peoples of Indo-China to decide their future by self-determination. Thus, when the atomic bombs dropped on Hiroshima and Nagasaki brought about an unexpectedly abrupt end to the war in the region, the communists were sufficiently well armed and in control of events to establish the Democratic Republic of Vietnam, with its capital at Hanoi.

The new republic was declared on 2 September 1945. But in July that year the Allies had agreed at Potsdam that France would regain its Indo-Chinese possessions. France was in no position to do so in August 1945, and so in September British and nationalist Chinese forces occupied the south and north of the country respectively. The size of their task was such that, by October 1945, the British had found it necessary to re-arm some of the surrendered Japanese units in order for them to act as a paramilitary police force in the south of the country. The British force comprised the 26,000 men of Major General D. Gracey's battle-hardened 20th Indian Division, plus air force and additional artillery support. But whereas the Chinese were content to deal with the Japanese without affecting the new régime in Hanoi, the British were firmly committed to return Indo-China to French control. Accordingly, on 5 October 1945 a French Expeditionary Corps, 21,500 strong and led by General Leclerc, entered Saigon and began the process of relieving the British forces, who handed over their temporary stewardship of southern Indo-China to the French on 9 October. In the months prior to and after the British withdrawal there was much political manoeuvring, and several violent confrontations between the communists, nationalists, French forces, French colonists, Gaullists, former Vichy supporters and forces and other disparate groups occurred. During this turbulent period various potentially workable compromises emerged, although none were acceptable to Paris. One such was Ho Chi Minh's agreement to the stationing of 25,000 French and French-officered Vietnamese troops in the major urban areas (to be followed by a French withdrawal in five annual stages, with completion in 1952), in return for French recognition of the Democratic Republic of Vietnam as a free state within both an Indo-Chinese Federation and the French Union.

The situation degenerated with each passing month, as two diametrically opposed philosophies and forces moved towards open conflict in early 1946. First of all there were the French, determined to retain control of French Indo-

China at all costs. Second, there were the communists, inspired by a charismatic leader committed to establish an independent, communist-dominated Vietnamese republic. Although the motivation used by Ho Chi Minh was initially anti-colonialist, and then nationalist, there is little doubt that a communist state was always his ultimate goal throughout the war that was about to commence

A major amphibious landing had been carried out by the French at Haiphong in the Red River delta on 6 March 1946, and the always uneasy relationship between the French and the newly established government in Hanoi deteriorated rapidly, against a backdrop of small-scale armed clashes. The landing by large elements of the French Expeditionary Corps on 6 March had added thousands on troops to the 150,000 nationalist Chinese troops and Viet Minh forces already in the area of the Red River delta. For the local population the significance of this was dramatic, because the 1945 rice harvest had been very poor, and even before the arrival of these armies they were literally starving. Consequently, the Red River delta was particularly receptive to any action that might expel the French and Chinese occupiers.

Then, on 19 December, the Viet Minh struck French positions around Hanoi with artillery, mortar and small-arms fire, which severed the city's electricity and water supplies. Shortly after this the guerrillas withdrew to their bases in the swamps and mountains of Tonkin and the area of the Chinese border. From there they prepared to conduct a classic revolutionary war in accordance with the principles expounded by Mao Tse-tung, whose own communist revolutionary war against the nationalist Chinese armies to the north was proceeding successfully.

Over the next three years the Viet Minh carried out numerous ambushes of French supply columns and attacks on isolated forts, as well as various acts of terrorism. Although the French forces (following the pattern of their colonial strategy of former times) were dispersed throughout the country, the main area of conflict was to the north of the country, in Tonkin. During those first years after the French return, the Foreign Legion bore the brunt of the attacks, and it continued to do so throughout France's post-1945 involvement with Indo-China.

Significant numbers of men from many different countries had found themselves in the armed forces of the losing side in the recently ended Second World War, and – having lost everything in that great conflict or being unable to adjust to their much-changed personal circumstances in the turmoil of the post-1945 world – many of them had found a new home and *raison d'être* in the Legion. These legionnaires were now engaged very directly in France's attempt to regain and maintain control of its territories in Indo-China. Although but one of hundreds of similar clashes, the particular nature of the Legion's war in Indo-China was characterised by the defence of the outpost at Phu Tong Hoa by a company of the 3e Régiment Étranger d'Infanterie (3 REI), which took place on 25 July 1948. The small fort – with defences constructed in the main of sandbags, logs, wire, bunkers and entrenchments – lay astride the strategically important road that ran between Hanoi and the Chinese border. Soon after nightfall, the first salvo of mortar bombs exploded across the position. This presaged a sustained, heavy and accurate mortar bombardment which soon breached the defensive perimeter fence. The small company of legionnaires – less than 100 strong – was considerably outnumbered, and the Viet Minh attackers eventually overran more than half of the base. Despite this the legionnaires continued to fight on, both within and from the fort, until a relief force arrived three days later. By that stage, twenty-one legionnaires, including the two most senior officers, had been killed. Nevertheless, with a flair that has throughout its history typified the *esprit de corps* of the élite organisation to which they belonged, as the relief column reached the entrance to the outpost it found the forty surviving legionnaires of the garrison paraded in their best uniforms. As the reinforcements drove into the battered fort, these forty men who had just fought a desperate three-day battle to ensure that Phu Tong Hoa remained in French hands, snapped to attention and presented arms in accordance with time-honoured military tradition.

Such incidents were frequent and typical both of the nature of the Legion and of the war that it, together with the other French Union forces, was required to fight for France in Indo-China. Meanwhile, in an ill-disguised attempt to placate the nationalists in particular, but also the communists, while at the same time installing a ruler who would be entirely under French control, in April 1948 Paris had established the discredited former Emperor Bao Dai as the emperor of an

Below: Ho Chi Minh (second left) and General Giap (right) at an operational planning meeting.

independent Vietnam. Not surprisingly the Viet Minh leadership was unimpressed by this, and in February 1950, following a successful attack on the French outpost at Lao Cai on the Red River close to the Chinese border (an event which coincided with Mao's victory in China and the prospect of significant quantities of Chinese aid[5] for the Viet Minh in the future), Giap and Ho felt sufficiently confident to move their guerrilla campaign into the counter-offensive phase.[6]

Early in 1950 Giap had at his disposal two infantry divisions, plus heavy mortars and anti-aircraft guns; but by the end of that year he had increased the strength of his regular forces to three divisions, and (nominally) to six divisions by the end of 1951.[7] Indeed, by 1954 the Viet Minh forces outnumbered the French Union forces. Throughout the war the French underestimated the Viet Minh capability, but two other important factors also affected French hopes and perceptions. First, the post-Roosevelt administration of President Truman, fuelled by McCarthyism and anti-communist sentiments in the United States – much reinforced by the North Korean invasion of South Korea in June 1950 – all indicated the possibility of American military support for the French cause. Second, the French government hoped that the National Assembly in Paris would authorise the deployment of conscripts to Indo-China, which would alleviate the chronic shortage of French troops and the consequent reliance upon regular units, the Legion and volunteers to serve there. But although America's eventual post-1954 military involvement in Vietnam was massive, it never used its significant combat power to assist the French. Similarly, the use of conscripts to fight beyond metropolitan France was never sanctioned by the National Assembly; a decision much influenced by a disaster that befell the French forces in Tonkin in the early autumn of 1950.

In mid-September, just six weeks before the PLA launched its devastating offensive against the UN forces in Korea, Giap struck the French forces in north-east Tonkin. The Viet Minh operations began with a series of assaults against French positions on the Cao Bang–Lang Son ridge, where the full weight of their offensive fell upon the French position at Dong Khe on 16 September 1950.

Dong Khe was a forward outpost of the Legion, set high in the jungle-clad, mist-shrouded hills that lay along Tonkin's border with China. The position was manned by some 260 men, comprising two companies of the 3 REI. The communist attack began with a heavy and accurate mortar barrage, followed during the next two days by further mortar bombardments interspersed with human wave attacks by more than 2,000 infantrymen. Time and again the attackers overran the perimeter defences and engaged in savage close combat with the legionnaires. Time and again they were forced to withdraw. But the final outcome of the battle was not in doubt, and at the end of the second day only a few of the surviving legionnaires had managed to escape from the shattered outpost. The significance of this battle extended well beyond the loss of a single outpost.

The fort at Dong Khe had previously been designated as the rendezvous for a French column that was already moving towards it from the small town of Cao Bang, about fifteen miles away. The column's mission was to evacuate and escort the anti-communist civilian population of Cao Bang to safety, and in view of what transpired Giap must have already been aware of the particular significance of Dong Khe. Indeed, the outpost was critical to the safety of the French column, and the 1er Bataillon Étranger de Parachutistes (1 BEP) plus a large force of Moroccan troops – a total of some 5,000 men – tried unsuccessfully to recapture it. But this force was ambushed in the Coc Xa valley by as many as 30,000 Viet Minh guerrillas. Despite the gallantry and discipline of the legionnaires during a battle that lasted for more than two weeks, the force was gradually overwhelmed and, with the Moroccans' morale on the verge of collapse, on 9 October the order came to break out of the valley. Only a handful of legionnaires and a number of terrified Moroccan soldiers managed to escape from the horrific few hours of fighting that ensued. The disaster was compounded shortly afterwards when the fleeing Moroccans reached the approaching column from Cao Bang, where their fear speedily infected the Moroccan troops of that force. At that moment the Viet Minh attacked the main column. The result was a massacre on a grand scale, one of the worst military defeats in French colonial history, which by 17 October left the Viet Minh in undisputed control of the border region and the principal supply routes into Tonkin from China. In the fighting about and between Dong Khe and Cao Bang the French lost about 7,000 men dead or as prisoners. The force had originally numbered about 10,000 in all. The recently formed 1 BEP was almost annihilated, and only about a dozen of its paratroopers survived. These men eventually reached the safety of the main French positions to the south, led by the battalion's adjutant, Captain Pierre Jeanpierre.[8]

Quite apart from the huge number of French casualties, the weapons and equipment lost were particularly significant, as they were quickly turned against their former owners. The Viet Minh haul included thirteen artillery weapons, 125 mortars, more than 900 machine-guns, 1,200 automatic rifles, 8,000 rifles and about 450 trucks. In Paris and throughout France the government and people were appalled by the disaster; and without hesitation a law was passed to prevent the hundreds of young Frenchmen conscripted for military service each year from being sent to areas in which military operations were taking place, or to take part in them other than in time of war. Three and a half years later, the existence of this legislation meant that the French Union forces were unable to generate the force levels necessary to prosecute their campaign in Indo-China effectively, or in sufficient strength to ensure the viability, relief or reinforcement of the operation at Dien Bien Phu. This new law also provided the communists with an important propaganda weapon, as they were able to cite the French government's disregard for the lives of its North African colonial troops and those of the Foreign Legion, as opposed to those of the indigenous European Frenchmen. As 1950 drew to a close, the morale of the population in France and its supporters in Indo-China reached its lowest point since the return of French troops to Indo-China almost exactly five years earlier.

But Giap's resounding victory in north-east Tonkin bred a degree of over-confidence and imprudence on the part of the communists, as the Viet Minh decided to advance their strategic campaign and engage the French on conventional battlefields. This decision coincided with the arrival of General Jean de Lattre de Tassigny as the French High Commissioner and Commander-in-Chief in Indo-China. He was a highly capable commander who concentrated his forces – even at the expense of the security of the southern parts of Vietnam, in Annam and Cochin China – and from January to June 1951 he used the superior French technology, fire-power and control of the air to inflict significant losses on the Viet Minh during their new offensive in the Red River delta. De Tassigny devised a strategy of creating fortified bases deep within Viet Minh territory, which Giap was then forced to attack. This brought the Viet Minh into killing areas for the French artillery and air-power, where the communists incurred substantial losses at little or no cost to the French garrisons. But for both sides this modern form of attrition warfare demanded large quantities of manpower – for the communists to replace their casualties and for the French to maintain the momentum of their strategy – and while Giap more or less managed to replace his losses, the requests for additional manpower that de Tassigny sent to Paris were hardly addressed, so that only a fraction of the reinforcements he needed actually arrived in Indo-China. Despite this handicap, the operational concepts developed by de Tassigny continued to appeal to the French high command, and their later application to the north-east of the Plaine des Jarres in 1954 precipitated the great battle that finally ended the French presence in Indo-China.

On the first occasion that Giap's forces clashed with de Tassigny's, at Vinh Yen from 13 to 17 January 1951, the communist 308th and 312th Divisions – 22,000 strong in all – lost between 6,000 and 9,000 dead, with 8,000 wounded, and 600 men taken prisoner. They had been opposed by only 8,000 French soldiers, but these troops were supported by a generous allocation of air-power, and the liberal use of napalm destroyed the concentrated Viet Minh units. Subsequently, the communists also suffered serious defeats at Mao Khe in March, where Giap lost 3,000 casualties in three days, and at Phat Diem (the Day River) in June, where they sustained a further 11,000 casualties. Meanwhile, General de Tassigny protected the Tonkinese capital, Hanoi, with a chain of forts (the de Lattre Line) and maintained a formidable mobile reserve, comprised of para-troops, armoured and amphibious units and vehicle-borne infantry, to deal with any attacks against the French outposts.

In turn de Lattre's successes and improving French morale bred over-confidence on their side. In mid-November 1951 a major operation designed to take the initiative from the communists and start the process of destroying their bases and infrastructure began, but it was then abandoned the following February, when a garrison of paratroops and other units at the newly established base of Hoa Binh was forced to withdraw in the face of six Viet Minh divisions which had cut off the base. But by then General Raoul Salan had replaced de Tassigny as the French commander in Indo-China,[9] and it soon became obvious that the lessons of Cao Bang–Lang Son and Hoa Binh – the dangers of over-extended lines of communication, isolated garrisons, inadequate reserves, a dependence upon air support and (above all else) underestimating the enemy – had not been well learnt by the French.

The next blow came as soon as the 1952 monsoon ended in October. It fell on the French positions at the Nghia Lo ridge, astride the ground between the Red River and the Black River to the north-west of Hanoi. Here, the communist 308th, 312th and 316th Divisions sought to destroy the French outposts at Nghia Lo and Gia Hoi, prior to a major assault on the strategically vital Red River delta. First, the 308th Division overwhelmed the Nghia Lo garrison, from which onslaught only a few survivors escaped, covered by a near-suicidal – but none the less effective – paratroop assault. Giap's forces enjoyed similar successes elsewhere, and by 17 October they controlled the important Nghia Lo ridge.

An attempt by General Salan to turn the communist gains to French advantage failed, when a counter-offensive (Operation 'Lorraine') by some 30,000 soldiers in armoured, amphibious, engineer and airborne units became over-extended. Giap managed to draw the French ever farther into the jungle and despite the capture by the French of considerable quantities of Viet Minh *matériel* – including a number of Soviet-supplied trucks – the French high command ordered an end to the operation on 14 November. A familiar pattern then emerged as the French sustained some 1,200 casualties between 17 November and 24 November, during their withdrawal along the roads and tracks that were constantly ambushed from the dense jungle and hills that surrounded them. Salan's Operation 'Lorraine' proved to be a costly venture for the French and there was a real need for a new strategic initiative. The political and military pressure from Paris to develop and mount a war-winning operation in the protracted conflict was becoming irresistible.

Throughout the war, despite the French military presence along the length and breadth of Indo-China, the main focus of conflict was always in Tonkin and northern Vietnam; specifically in the border areas and the Red River delta to the south of Hanoi. In late 1952 the French Union forces achieved a success reminiscent of those of early 1951, when a well-defended base at Na San, close to the border with Laos, not only defeated all Giap's attempts to overrun it, but also forced the Viet Minh to concentrate their forces and so made them vulnerable to air attack.[10] The communists suffered enormous losses, and this had prompted a revival of interest in the concept of forcing the Viet Minh to conduct a conventional battle on ground of French choosing, so that the full weight of French fire- and air-power could be brought to bear.

Coincidentally, the whole focus of the French campaign had moved towards the Vietnam–Laos border during the early months of 1953, when the Viet Minh invaded Laos that April. By May 1953 the French had deployed troops to new forward bases within Laos at Luang Prabang, Muong Khoua and on the Plaine des Jarres, with the task of interdicting the invading Viet Minh units. In fact, Giap's intentions were to seize the Laotian opium crop and to tie in his operations with those of the communist Pathet Lao guerrillas in furtherance of his long-term strategy; but in practice it was the French response to this invasion that initiated a chain of events which would ultimately decide the outcome of the entire war just a year later.

Soon after Giap's incursion into Laos, General Henri Navarre replaced Salan as French commander in Indo-China. Despite having 190,000 men at his disposal, and a potentially useful Vietnamese national army in embryo, Navarre's forces, with their country-wide security remit, were overstretched even before their deployment into Laos and they were now more thinly spread than ever. As 1953 drew on, Navarre reviewed his options for the future conduct of the campaign. His considerations were driven by four imperatives. There was the need to create and maintain a viable mobile reserve, the need to isolate the Viet Minh forces in Laos, the need to maintain control of the Red River delta – the key to Hanoi and the vital port of Haiphong, and finally there was the need to reduce the overall level or scale of French static commitments throughout Indo-China. The last of these was dependent upon forcing the Viet Minh to concentrate their forces into fewer areas. This in turn meant that the French had to seize the operational initiative in order to drive strategic events. Navarre was also under constant political pressure from Paris to create 'military conditions favourable to a resolution of the conflict' and so end what had become, within France, an extremely unpopular foreign war. Central to these considerations was the fact of the Viet Minh presence in Laos, and their consequent need to move regularly between Tonkin and Laos.

Inevitably, therefore, General Navarre's eyes were drawn towards the main Viet Minh transit route into Laos: from Tuan Giao in Tonkin to the Nam Ou valley in Laos. This was the route that the Viet Minh 312th Division had followed during its invasion of Laos in April. En route it had crossed into Laos just after passing through a large village and airstrip sited in the middle of a wide, flat valley surrounded by the jungle-clad hills of the T'ai Mountains. The name of this otherwise unremarkable village was soon destined to be as familiar to the citizens of France as that of Paris, Calais or Marseilles. Although the local population knew the village at the valley centre as Muong Thanh, the name by which it was to become known internationally was Dien Bien Phu.

# 2
# THE OPERATIONAL AND STRATEGIC DEBATE

On 30 November 1952 the French Union forces stationed in the Dien Bien Phu valley had been evacuated in the face of a significant threat to the area that was then posed by the Viet Minh 316th Division and Independent Regiment No. 148. While the forced withdrawal from Dien Bien Phu was downplayed by the French high command in Hanoi at the time, it had in fact provided the Viet Minh with an unimpeded route between Tonkin and Laos and also meant that the communists controlled the T'ai region of the country: where much of the indigenous population had long supported the French. Therefore, although the later conflict in the valley has traditionally – but over-simplistically – been attributed primarily to a French desire to bring the Viet Minh to battle on French terms, this operational goal had undoubtedly been preceded by the strategic imperative for the French to regain control of Dien Bien Phu and the surrounding area at the earliest opportunity. A failure to do so would be tantamount to writing-off Laos to communist control. This need had been stated in early January 1953 by the French commander in Indo-China, General Raoul Salan, in Operational Directive No. 40: which ordered an operation on 10 January with a view to recapturing Dien Bien Phu and regaining control of the T'ai province. His intention was for the recaptured base to then assume the role of a blocking position between Tonkin and Laos, while providing an anchor for long-range patrols and commando operations to be conducted throughout the surrounding territory. However, because of competing commitments elsewhere in Indo-China (including Operation 'Lorraine' and the fight at Na San) and the continued lack of available troops and resources, this operation never took place.

But the importance of Dien Bien Phu – lying as it did astride the principal route into and out of Laos – had been firmly imprinted upon the consciousness of the military staff in Saigon: a staff already convinced of the efficacy of using well-established strong-points – 'fortified hedgehogs' – to bring the communists to battle on ground of French choosing, and then to use superior fire-power (particularly air-delivered) to inflict heavy casualties on the enemy at minimal risk to the French Union forces. Although General Salan left Indo-China in the summer of 1953, he had already ensured that the strategic and operational significance of that valley in faraway north-west Tonkin had been registered by the appropriate government ministers in Paris as well as by those in positions of influence at General Headquarters in Saigon. And right up to his final days in Indo-China, Salan continued to advocate most strongly the merits of the use of the fortified hedgehogs. So it was that when, on 28 May 1953, Lieutenant General Henri Navarre inherited responsibility for an increasingly unpopular war, he also inherited what must at first sight have seemed an attractive but as yet unfulfilled concept for dominating the T'ai region and at the same time dealing the Viet Minh a blow that would redress some of the war-weariness and cynicism then prevalent in Paris. Notwithstanding his overall professional competence and intellect, however, Navarre was inexperienced in the way of warfare in Indo-China. So it is possible that he was more susceptible than might otherwise have been the case to the enthusiasm of the staff officers he inherited (although he soon replaced many with his own appointees) for Salan's concept of operations and ideas concerning the future role of Dien Bien Phu. One of Navarre's appointees as his deputy chief of staff (operations), Colonel Louis Berteil, was a particular advocate of the widespread application of the fortified base concept, and this officer may have had a significant influence upon Navarre's later thinking concerning Dien Bien Phu. In any event, during his first month in post, Navarre apparently weighed the facts and came to the conclusion that the concept of air-supplied bases deep within enemy-held territory did indeed afford the limited number of troops under his command a means of dominating large areas of ground.

In mid-June 1953 he focused his attention directly upon the T'ai region and the Dien Bien Phu valley, when the commander of French Union ground forces in northern Vietnam, Major General René Cogny, proposed that Dien Bien Phu should not only be re-occupied as an anchor position from which to provide military support for the mobile operations of locally-based T'ai forces, but that it could also eventually become the T'ai regional capital in place of Lai Chau: which town he considered to be indefensible. Such a move was politically attractive to Saigon, as it would allow the T'ai leader, Deo Van Long, to counter-balance the influence of the Viet Minh in the key strategic area adjacent to the Laotian border.[11] Finally, Cogny and Navarre were in agreement that despite its military role in late 1952, Na San had by mid-1953 become operationally largely irrelevant, and could safely be abandoned if a new base were established at Dien Bien Phu.

Although subsequent inquiries, claims and counter-claims post-May 1954 indicate that Navarre and Cogny had in their own minds accorded an operation at Dien Bien Phu different purposes and degrees of emphasis, it is irrefutable that the broad principle of launching a force to recapture the valley was agreed in Hanoi on or about 16 June 1953. On 17 July General Navarre presented his overall operational plan for the next twelve months to the Joint Chiefs of Staff in Paris, and on 24 July he briefed the government's National Defence Committee. Among the recriminations that took place a year later, after the battle of Dien Bien Phu had been fought and lost, the extent of the specific commitment to occupy Dien Bien Phu that was expressed at these high-level briefings remained unclear; although the operation was certainly not accorded the profile or level of discussion that it perhaps deserved. It is a matter of record that on 25 July the military staff in Saigon issued Operational Directive No. 563, which provided for the occupation of Dien Bien Phu in order to inhibit the Viet Minh threat to and from northern Laos.

Just over two weeks later, on 12 August, the base at Na San was successfully evacuated; which released some 9,000 men – nine infantry battalions – and the air-power that had supported the garrison for use elsewhere. Thus Na San continued to feature prominently in the saga of Dien Bien Phu; for its successful defence in 1952 vindicated the hedgehog concept, while its long-term operational irrelevance prompted its evacuation (which required the substitute occupation of Dien Bien Phu). Finally, the success of that evacuation by air led many French military planners later to assume that, *in extremis*, a base at Dien Bien Phu could always be evacuated in like fashion. In June the decision had been taken in-theatre. In July, that plan had been, if not entirely exposed and unequivocally endorsed, at least not opposed by Paris. Then, in August, the evacuation of Na San made the call for an operation at Dien Bien Phu irresistible. But the die was finally cast on 22 October, when France concluded a major treaty with Laos, which dealt principally with the future independent status of Laos within the French Union, but none the less implied that a defence obligation had been placed upon Paris as the price of the Laotian government's signature. This meant that the security of northern Laos and the need to dominate the routes between Laos and northern Vietnam had now assumed an even greater significance than that which had obtained previously. Consequently, the Franco–Laotian treaty set the final seal upon the matter, and the militarily desirable operation, which had subsequently become strategically inevitable, had finally become politically unavoidable.

The shades of language and perception used much later by Navarre and Cogny in order to justify and excuse their actions in respect of Dien Bien Phu were complex and revealed ambiguities that filled many volumes of military, legal and

**NORTHERN FRENCH INDO-CHINA IN 1953–54**

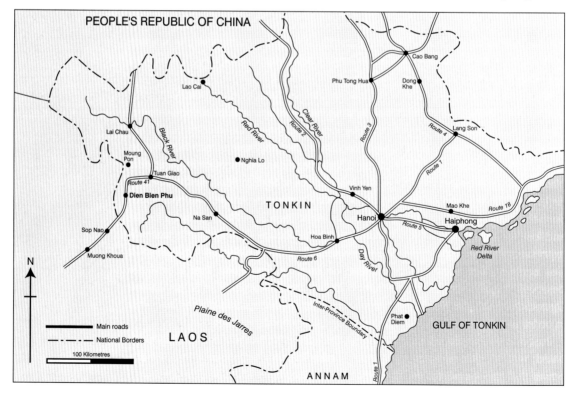

non-legal documents, letters, reports and inquiries. But in simple terms, Navarre's view of Dien Bien Phu (and that of many of his staff in Saigon) was that of a permanently occupied, heavily fortified base, at which the Viet Minh could be forced into a set-piece battle and destroyed by the superior air- and fire-power of the French Union forces. And there is no doubt that he was influenced very significantly by the role of France as *de facto* guarantor, since 22 October, of the future security of the whole of Laos. Cogny, however, envisaged Dien Bien Phu primarily as a focus for mobile and commando operations which would dominate the area and take the war to the Viet Minh through aggressive patrolling; while the main base would exist to sustain these activities and provide a rallying-point and focus for the French in the T'ai region. The staff of his headquarters, with its responsibility for the operational command of all French Union ground forces in northern Vietnam, undoubtedly shared and supported Cogny's perception of the probable future role of Dien Bien Phu.

Although Navarre took considerable time and trouble to visit all areas of his command, and received extensive briefings on all aspects of the conflict, his approach to the war betrayed his professional and intellectual background as a European soldier and staff officer. Furthermore, even though he had been involved in counter-guerrilla operations during pre-Second World War campaigns in North Africa and Syria, and had extensive experience of military intelligence work, he had no experience of warfare in Indo-China. Cogny, on the other hand, was much clearer about what could and could not be achieved at Dien Bien Phu. These fundamental differences of perception between two generals who should have been absolutely within each other's minds would eventually prove fatal for the thousands of French Union troops who would fight and die in that far off fertile valley and the jungle-clad hills that surrounded it. In many ways, the almost 1,000 kilometres that lay between their respective headquarters emphasised the distance between their personal views of the impending operation.

Events now moved ahead apace. Navarre's headquarters in Saigon issued Operational Directive No. 852 to Major General Cogny's headquarters in Hanoi on 2 November, which established the command and control arrangements and outline organisation of troops to task for the operation. It also appointed Cogny overall commander of the operation, which was to be carried out not later than 1 December. This document alerted his staff to the real implications of that which they were now required to accomplish, and in short order they provided Cogny with a comprehensive response to Navarre's directive; indicating a number of basic flaws in the concept and timing of the operation. They also proposed later that the Red River delta to the south of Hanoi should be the focus of main effort, rather than the T'ai region.

The extent of Cogny's disagreement with Navarre's directive seems strange, given their broad agreement of mid-June, but quite apart from their diverging views of the primary role of Dien Bien Phu, it is likely that Cogny had not envisaged such an early move into the valley. He had probably expected a greater degree of personal control over the timing of the operation. The early divergence between Navarre and Cogny on this issue had widened during the period of Navarre's visit to Paris during July, and – the modern military communications of the time notwithstanding – the geographical separation between Saigon and Hanoi no doubt hampered the two generals' day-to-day ability to establish common parameters for such a major operation mounted at relatively short notice. The points raised by Cogny's staff might also have been an attempt to place their professional misgivings on record, in anticipation of the political, military and media witch-hunt following a battlefield reverse that has increasingly bedevilled military decision-makers and commanders at all levels ever since the Second World War. Following the military collapse of France in 1940, their relatively recent experience of French history probably weighed heavily on the minds of several senior officers in Hanoi.

Despite the controversy surrounding Navarre's directive, Cogny accepted the mission by default – at no time did he consider that it was a resignation issue – and Navarre set 20 November as the date on which the operation was to begin. On 11 and 12 November Cogny briefed his airborne and air force commanders, and the thrust of his orders to the commander of the paratroop units, Brigadier General Jean Gilles, indicated his continued belief (or intention, irrespective of Navarre's concept!) that Dien Bien Phu would be a patrol-support base, rather than the fortified strong-point that Navarre clearly expected it to be.

The decision to transfer the government of the T'ai Federation from Lai Chau had been taken on 4 November; on the 13th Lieutenant Colonel Trancart, the French commander in Lai Chau, to the north of Dien Bien Phu, was informed of the impending operation, and that his force of 2,101 men would in due course be required to abandon the town and join the forces shortly to arrive at Dien Bien Phu. Trancart immediately set in train the withdrawal of the 700 men of his 1er Groupement Mobile de Partisans T'ai (GMPT 1) to Dien Bien Phu in anticipation of the French airborne landing. This evacuation and relocation to Dien Bien Phu was allocated the code-name 'Pollux' and the subsequent fate of the larger part of the garrison and many civilians of Lai Chau would later bear significantly upon the future of Dien Bien Phu. Navarre's particular preoccupation with the security of Laos, the political aspects of the move of the T'ai political centre of gravity from Lai Chau to Dien Bien Phu, and the command and control co-ordination arrangements between Cogny in Hanoi and Colonel Boucher de Crèvecoeur, the commander of French Union forces in Laos, were emphasised and detailed in a final operational directive issued on 14 November. On the same day, the French National Defence Council had, belatedly, circulated a note to the appropriate ministers in Paris suggesting that Navarre might wish to re-visit the plan briefed to it on 24 July. It is unclear whether this reflected a considered re-assessment of Navarre's plans by Paris or was merely another attempt to forestall any later criticism of the government in the event of a military failure in Indo-China. In any event, this note was apparently ignored by ministers, as were the potential implications and pitfalls of the impending operation.

In the meantime French intelligence reports on 17 November indicated the presence of elements of the Viet Minh Independent Regiment No. 148 in an area that had previously been assessed as devoid of Viet Minh troops. Other reports also provided early evidence of the movement elsewhere, but possibly towards the T'ai region, of units of four of the five communist divisions as part of a major re-deployment of General Vo Nguyen Giap's People's Army of Vietnam (PAVN). While the presence of some Viet Minh troops in the valley would not necessarily prejudice the success of the planned assault by six élite battalions of French paratroops, the operational-level movement of major formations of the Viet Minh regular forces would certainly bear directly upon the longer-term future of Dien Bien Phu; and upon whether that future would eventually prove to be the one envisaged by General Navarre or that of Major General Cogny.

In any event, the airborne operation remained scheduled for 20 November; just three days away. By 17 November, whatever the longer term role of Dien Bien Phu might turn out to be, for the 4,560 paratroops of six airborne battalions – the vast majority of whom, for security reasons, still had no knowledge of their destination – a significant change in the weather was now the only thing that could prevent their drop into the valley of Dien Bien Phu on Friday, 20 November 1953.

**The Battleground**

The Dien Bien Phu valley is situated about fourteen kilometres east of the Laotian border, and is almost 300 kilometres from Hanoi, the principal city of Tonkin and northern Vietnam. The valley covered about 120 square kilometres, with a perimeter that was roughly eighty kilometres in length. At its centre lay the village of Dien Bien Phu – or Muong Thanh – and scattered about the valley were several smaller villages, hamlets and isolated dwellings. The valley's main access to the outside world was Provincial Route No. 41, which generally supported movement by suitably robust vehicles during all but the monsoon months. A complementary vehicle track – the Pavie Track – ran the length of the valley to the west of and parallel with Route 41, although it generally became unusable by wheeled vehicles in bad weather and in any case petered out and became impassable to all vehicles about three kilometres to the south of Muong Thanh village. Route 41 was the principal road between Tonkin and northern Laos; it also lay astride the main through route from China and Burma into northern Indo-China, and as such had long been of commercial and strategic importance. Much of the valley was cultivated – predominantly as rice paddy – and the Nam-Youm River flowing through it provided irrigation which ensured its continued fertility. A propensity to flood during the annual monsoon was reflected in the precautionary construction of many of the 112 traditional village dwellings on raised terraces or stilts. An exception to this standard type of building was the small cluster of European-style stone buildings at Muong Thanh which had been occupied by a junior French colonial administrator since the early years of the 20th century, and prior to the Japanese occupation in 1945. These houses had been built on some of the higher ground adjacent to

Muong Thanh village. As the use of aeroplanes became a more usual means of travel in the first part of the century, a small airstrip had been cleared in the 1920s and this lay a short distance to the north of the village. This facility was subsequently improved for military use by the Japanese during March and April 1945. The importance of this airstrip continued after 1945, and the need to maintain its viability and security was a critical factor in planning the operation at Dien Bien Phu in late 1953.

Dotted about the valley were a few low, brush-covered hills, which with very few exceptions rose no higher than 470 metres. Immediately beyond the edge of the valley bottom was a line of hills broken by steep re-entrants, all of which exceeded 500 metres in height and some of which were more than 550 metres high. The distance from this high ground to the airstrip at Muong Thanh was only about four kilometres; and the next line of surrounding hills, which in this case rose to about 1,100 metres, was only a further four to five kilometres away from the airstrip. These densely forested and jungle-clad ridges overlooked the entire valley, and quickly gave way to the even higher mountain ranges that lay beyond them.[12]

From the outset, the key to control of the valley and its main airstrip at Muong Thanh was undoubtedly the ability to dominate the high ground which surrounded the Dien Bien Phu valley; at least to a distance that exceeded the maximum range of any artillery that an enemy could emplace there. But the artillery intelligence staff of the French high command dismissed this vital factor with its assessment that the Viet Minh artillery had not the range to engage the valley from reverse slope positions beyond the hills, and that it could not be emplaced within range of Dien Bien Phu on the forward slopes where it would certainly be observed and speedily destroyed by the superior French artillery or by air attack. Consequently, an ability to control directly the high ground surrounding Dien Bien Phu was by no means essential. This gross underestimation of the Viet Minh military capability was only exceeded by its over-estimation of the capability of the French Union forces: especially their fire- and air-power. But the assumed superiority of French fire-power on the ground coupled with aerial dominance would be core features of the 'fortified hedgehog' operation that General Navarre certainly envisaged would take place at Dien Bien Phu from late 1953, even though he had yet to articulate his concept for this particular operation fully or unambiguously.

Below: French Union activities within the Dien Bien Phu valley could all too easily be observed from the surrounding hills and mountains. Here, paratroopers move past one of the several hamlets that lay in the valley, their patrol constantly in view from the nearby high ground.

# 3

# OPENING MOVES

## NOVEMBER 1953 – MARCH 1954

**The Airborne Assault 20–23 November**

0630 hours on Friday 20 November 1953. A C-47 ('Dakota') transport aircraft circled lazily above a dense bank of fog that shrouded the valley of Dien Bien Phu. Only the highest peaks of the surrounding hills protruded starkly from the rolling mass of grey fog that blanketed the ground. The aircraft had taken off from the Bach-Mai military airbase at Hanoi at 0530, and the mission of its occupants was critical to what was now code-named Operation 'Castor'. Inside the C-47 were Brigadier General Jean Gilles, the commander of French airborne units in Indo-China, Brigadier General Jean Dechaux, commander of French air force tactical operations in Indo-China, and Lieutenant General Pierre Bodet, the French deputy commander-in-chief in Indo-China. These men would decide whether or not the weather would permit the operation to proceed; if it were to be cancelled, Operation 'Castor' would almost certainly be overtaken by the competing resource and manpower needs of other operations, and would be postponed indefinitely. However, at about 0700 the fog began to lift, and at 0720 Major General Cogny in Hanoi received word from General Dechaux that Operation 'Castor' was viable. Cogny immediately passed the 'go' message to the paratroop units waiting with their sixty-five transport aircraft at Bach-Mai airfield, where they had been briefed during the early hours of that morning. At 0800 the aircraft engines roared into life and by 0815, with all aircraft airborne, the assault force turned westwards towards Dien Bien Phu. They arrived above the valley just after 1030, and at 1035 the first sticks of paratroopers tumbled out of their transport aircraft and floated down into – or near – their designated drop zones. The order of battle and other details of the French Union forces for the initial drop of Operation 'Castor' on Friday 20 November are shown in table 1.

Although some Viet Minh troops were known to be in the Dien Bien Phu area, the relatively brief battle that ensued on 20 November was rather more intense than the paratroops had anticipated. On landing they were confronted by a force of Viet Minh regular troops of the PAVN that included the headquarters and Battalion No. 910 of Independent Regiment No. 148, the support (or 'heavy') weapons Company No. 226 of the same regiment's Battalion No. 920, plus the support company of Artillery Regiment No. 675. These support companies were equipped with recoilless rifles and mortars. Finally, one company of Infantry Regiment No. 48 of the 320th Infantry Division was also in the valley, recovering from an earlier battle with French Union forces. All these units were conducting training and refurbishment in the area, so were not prepared to conduct a defensive battle and, fortunately for the paratroopers, they were widely dispersed throughout the valley. The communist troops gave a good account of themselves, inflicting casualties of eleven dead and fifty-two wounded, but they were gradually overwhelmed by the deluge of élite troops that had dropped literally on top of them and were forced to withdraw from the valley, leaving at

**Table 1 – 20 NOVEMBER 1953**

| French Unit Military Designation | English Title | Commander | Strength | Remarks |
|---|---|---|---|---|
| 6 BPC (6e Bataillon de Parachutistes Coloniaux) | 6th Colonial Airborne Battalion | Major Marcel 'Bruno' Bigeard | 651 | Jumped into north DZ Natasha at 1035 20 Nov. Withdrawn from Dien Bien Phu 11 Dec, but returned to reinforce the garrison 16 Mar 54. |
| 2/1 RCP (2e Bataillon, 1er Régiment de Chasseurs Parachutiste) | 2nd Battalion, 1st Airborne Light Infantry Regiment | Major Jean Bréchignac | 569 | Jumped into south DZ Simone at 1035 20 Nov. Withdrawn from Dien Bien Phu 11 Dec, but returned to reinforce the garrison 1 to 5 Apr 54. |
| 1 BPC (1er Bataillon de Parachutistes Coloniaux) | 1st Colonial Airborne Battalion | Major Jean Souquet | 722 | Jumped into DZ 'Natasha' 1430 20 Nov. Withdrawn from Dien Bien Phu 11 Dec, but elements returned to reinforce the garrison 3 to 5 May 54. |
| GAP 1 (1er Groupement Aéroporté) | HQ Airborne Battlegroup No. 1 | Lieutenant Colonel Fourcade | | Jumped into DZ Simone. The total complement of forces commanded by GAP 1 was 1827 men. |
| 17 CGP (17e Compagnie de Génie Parachutiste) | 17th Company Airborne Combat Engineers | | About 120 | Heavy equipment landed at south-west DZ Octavie. |
| 35 RALP (35e Régiment d'Artillerie Légère Parachutiste) | 35th Airborne Light Artillery Regiment | Major Jean Millot | Two batteries (eight 75mm guns, with about 80 personnel) | Heavy weapons and equipment landed at DZ Octavie. |

For simplicity, the usual French military practice of showing the abbreviated numerical designation of units with an 'e', 'er' or 're' suffix (e.g. 13e DBLE, 1er BEP, 1re CEPML) has not been adopted in this work. However, the appropriate suffixes that would otherwise apply to these abbreviated forms of unit designation are clearly indicated by reference to the full unit titles where shown. Similarly, in the interests of clarity, the usual French practice of using all lower case text for military unit designations when written in full has not been adopted. Finally, although 'parachutiste' translates literally as 'paratroop', 'airborne' (and in some cases 'parachute') has been adopted here and in the main text to reflect more closely the British and US military designations of their equivalent national airborne forces.

**Table 2 – 21 NOVEMBER 1953**

| French Unit Military Designation | English Title | Commander | Strength | Remarks |
|---|---|---|---|---|
| EDAP (Élément Division Aéroporté) | Tactical Command Element of an Airborne Division (supported by elements of the 342nd Airborne Signal Company) | General Jean Gilles | | By last light on 22 Nov, the total strength of forces about Dien Bien Phu commanded by EDAP was 4,560 men. EDAP was later relieved by Colonel Dominique Bastiani's Paratroop Operational Group (GOP – Groupement Opérationnel Parachutiste) once the valley had been secured. Finally, overall command of the force at Dien Bien Phu passed to the GONO (Groupement Opérationnel Nord-Ouest) and Colonel Christian de Castries on 7 Dec. |
| GAP 2 (2e Groupement Aéroporté) | HQ Airborne Battlegroup No. 2 | Lieutenant Colonel Pierre Langlais | | Most of the heavy drop equipment for the airborne assault force arrived at Octavie on 21 Nov. |
| 1 BEP (1er Bataillon Étranger de Parachutistes) | 1st Foreign Legion Airborne Battalion | Major Maurice Guiraud | 653 | Remained at Dien Bien Phu after initial phase of Operation 'Castor'. |
| 8 BPC (8e Bataillon de Parachutistes de Choc) | 8th Airborne Assault (or 'Shock') Battalion | Captain Pierre Tourret | 656 | Remained at Dien Bien Phu after initial phase of Operation 'Castor'. |
| 1 CEPML (1re Compagnie Étrangère Parachutiste de Mortiers Lourds) | 1st Foreign Legion Airborne Heavy Mortar Company | Lieutenant Jacques Molinier | 71 | Twelve 120mm mortars. Grouped with and under the control of 1 BEP, but fired missions in support of other units at Dien Bien Phu as necessary. |

least ninety dead and a number of weapons, documents and some equipment behind them. Within six hours of the initial landing, the French soldiers had secured the central area and the three main drop zones about Dien Bien Phu (Natasha, Simone and Octavie; DZ Suzanne to the south-west of the village was not activated), and the

**Table 3 – 22 NOVEMBER 1953**

| French Unit Military Designation | English Title | Commander | Strength | Remarks |
|---|---|---|---|---|
| 5 BPVN (5e Bataillon de Parachutistes Vietnamiens) | 5th Vietnamese Airborne Battalion | Major Bouvery | About 750 | Withdrawn from Dien Bien Phu 25 Jan, but returned to reinforce the garrison 14 Mar 54. In mid-Dec 5 BPVN was commanded by Major Leclerc. |

new base was ready for consolidation by subsequent parachute drops scheduled for 21 and 22 November. These later drops involved the headquarters, units and support organisations shown in tables 2 and 3.

Meanwhile, almost 100 kilometres to the north, the T'ai partisans of GMPT 1, under the command of Captain Bordier, had departed Lai Chau in accordance with Lieutenant Colonel Trancart's orders, as a precursor to Operation 'Pollux', and were already well on their way towards the valley. But within a couple of days' march from Dien Bien Phu, they began to encounter elements of Independent Regiment No. 148, which had been expelled by the Operation 'Castor' airborne assault from the area that GMPT 1 were now trying to reach.

A running battle ensued and, despite the fighting tenacity of the T'ai soldiers, on the morning of 23 November the 2/1 RCP was ordered to advance northwards to assist and link up with them. This they soon did at the village of Na Ten, about seven kilometres from Dien Bien Phu, and the T'ai force continued its march into the valley without further incident and in notably good order.

The removal of GMPT 1 from Lai Chau overland to Dien Bien Phu was without question a success, but for that very reason it created a dangerous precedent for the French high command, who would in due course order a T'ai rearguard of some 2,100 T'ai irregulars and thirty-six French soldiers to complete precisely the same journey almost a month later.

## French Union Force Development

Meanwhile, the build-up at Dien Bien Phu had continued. By 6 December three more units had arrived to complement, and in some cases relieve, the paratroop units that had carried out the initial airborne assault as shown in table 4.

The overall size and layout of the base already exceeded that necessary to support the type of patrol operations carried out by the regional

**Table 4 – ADDITIONAL FRENCH UNION FORCES AT DIEN BIEN PHU AS AT 6 DECEMBER 1953**

| French Unit Military Designation | English Title | Remarks |
|---|---|---|
| 3 BT (3e Bataillon T'ai) | 3rd T'ai Infantry Battalion | |
| BAAL (Batterie Autonome d'Artillerie Laotien) | Laotian Autonomous Artillery Battery | Equipped with eight 105mm guns. The BAAL landed at Dien Bien Phu 28 Nov, but was returned to Laos during Dec when relieved by other artillery units. |
| 3/31 BG (3e Compagnie du 31e Bataillon du Génie) | 3rd Company, 31st Engineer Battalion | Arrived at Dien Bien Phu 4 Dec. Enabled work to begin on up-rating the airstrip, roads and bridges. |

GMPT units, or those of the Groupements de Commandos Mixtes Aéroportés (GCMA)[13] – the French special forces units that operated against strategic targets deep within communist territory. But the tons of defence stores, engineer equipment, artillery, reserve ammunition and additional manpower necessary to transform Dien Bien Phu into an impregnable fortress were not yet in evidence; and as early as the final week of November 1953 – even though the fact probably passed unnoticed by most of the soldiers hard at work within the evolving garrison – Dien Bien Phu was already in the throes of an operational identity crisis, as the high command in Saigon and the northern Vietnam command in Hanoi continued to debate and formulate its future role.

### Misconceptions and Misunderstandings, November – December 1953

This less than ideal situation was exemplified by the ambiguities contained in two key operational directives: the first issued by Major General Cogny in Hanoi on 30 November and the second by General Navarre on 3 December. These two directives followed a visit by both generals to the new base on 29 November and presumably took account of their observations and discussions that day, although it has been suggested that the document issued from Saigon had been largely drafted by Colonel Berteil during Navarre's visit to Dien Bien Phu with Cogny, and that its final form therefore remained unaffected by that visit. The first document called for the security and uninhibited use of the Dien Bien Phu airstrip to be maintained, for long-range patrol operations or larger sorties to be mounted into the surrounding region by at least half the garrison at all times, and for the force based there to support the impending withdrawal of the T'ai and other French Union forces from Lai Chau. In broad terms, this was a charter for the establishment and maintenance of a patrol base, which could be evacuated by air if necessary, and which would enable the closure of the French presence at Lai Chau. All of this more or less reflected Cogny's original perception of the role of Dien Bien Phu, but the scale and tempo of external operations and the need to defend the new base could not be achieved by those units that had parachuted in or air-landed there between 20 and 30 November. Cogny's directive meant that the base would need significant reinforcement by units organised and equipped on heavier scales than those of the paratroop battalions. Dien Bien Phu would need a considerable amount of additional artillery firepower and the reserves of ammunition to support it. Finally, a very great deal of engineer work would be required in order to meet the particular requirement for guaranteed air access and the level of defensive security for the base that this implied.

While Colonel Dominique Bastiani's Groupement Opérationnel Parachutiste (GOP) (which had assumed command of Dien Bien Phu from GAP 2 once the valley had been secured) set about the task of launching offensive and intelligence-gathering operations into the surrounding hills and jungle with considerable enthusiasm, the paratroopers were less well disposed to the preparation of the trenches, bunkers and field defences that occupied virtually all their time when they were back in the base. The engineer support and resources available for this exhausting work were minimal, and the unsuitability of paratroop units for this role must have been very evident both within and beyond the garrison. It is worth adding that Cogny had expressed to Navarre on 28 or 29 November his continued reservations about the security of the isolated base in light of the threat posed by the Viet Minh forces reportedly moving towards the north-west. He had requested additional mobile forces for an operation into the area north of the Red River, with a view to reducing and diluting the gathering threat to Dien Bien Phu. But General Navarre had not been persuaded by Cogny, and in any case he already had a plan of his own in mind for the use of any currently uncommitted forces.

The second key directive that affected the future role of Dien Bien Phu was that issued by General Navarre's headquarters in Saigon on 3 December. This made crystal clear Navarre's intention and decision to bring the Viet Minh to battle at Dien Bien Phu, which 'must be held at all costs', and the key role of the base as the focus of the French Union defence of 'the Northwest' – and therefore, by implication, not only of north-west Vietnam, but also of Laos. The intention to abandon Lai Chau was also included. But most importantly this directive out-lined Saigon's view of the Viet Minh capability and the probable course of the battle at Dien Bien Phu. It envisaged a period of several weeks during which the communists would manoeuvre their forces into the area. This would be followed by a couple of weeks of reconnaissance and deployment. Finally, the Viet Minh

Below: Operation Castor, 20 November 1953. The airborne assault.

would attack. This phase would last for several days and would end with the defeat of the Viet Minh offensive. This grossly over-optimistic assessment exemplified the French high command's persistent under-estimation of the Viet Minh capability during the war in Indo-China.

Meanwhile, General Navarre had clearly over-estimated the offensive and defensive capability of the position at Dien Bien Phu, and indeed of the wider French Union forces and resources available to him throughout Vietnam. Just a week later, on 12 December, he issued Operational Instruction No. 964, which directed the mounting of Operation 'Atlante': a major offensive in the central region of Vietnam during January 1954, involving up to forty-five infantry battalions and eight artillery battalions. Irrespective of the fact that the failure of the latter phases of Operation 'Atlante' resulted in the commitment of airborne forces already earmarked as dedicated reserves for Dien Bien Phu to retrieve the operational situation, the idea that the French Union forces could absorb and win two major operations at the same time underlined the extent to which Saigon had lost touch with the real capability of the forces at its disposal, and with that of the ever-growing communist forces which now opposed them.

In many respects, these two directives (together with that concerning Operation 'Atlante') encapsulated the failure of the French high command at Dien Bien Phu. For even a superficial review of these documents reveals the posit of an unachievable mission, an invalid appreciation of the terrain, an unrealistic allocation of troops to task, an under-estimation of the enemy and an over-estimation of own forces. Navarre's directive also laid the foundations of the later mystique attracted by Dien Bien Phu, where 'must be held at all

Below: Colonel de Castries (centre), the French commander at Dien Bien Phu, with Major General Cogny (right), the commander of French Union forces in Northern Vietnam, during a visit of the French minister of defence, M. René Pleven (left), to Dien Bien Phu on 19 February 1954.

costs' translated in the French military mind into a matter of duty, honour and – finally – supreme sacrifice. Nevertheless, the 'paper trail' that would decide the course of events at the valley of Dien Bien Phu over the next five months began with these two flawed and ambiguous documents.

**Operation 'Pollux': The Evacuation of Lai Chau**

The final withdrawal of the T'ai and remaining French Union forces from Lai Chau in accordance with the original concept for Operations 'Castor' and 'Pollux' – and as indicated by the directives of 30 November and 3 December – followed the total evacuation of the Lai Chau valley between 7 and 10 December. By then Lai Chau was facing a serious threat posed by the Viet Minh 316th Division. Once most of the French Union garrison and T'ai Federation government officials had been evacuated from the town by air, as much *matériel* as possible that might have been of use to the advancing communists was destroyed. The remaining T'ai light infantry irregular companies – ten in all, many with their families accompanying the locally engaged soldiers – set out for Dien Bien Phu. They soon encountered elements of the 316th Division and Independent Regiment No. 148. During the next ten days the T'ai soldiers became embroiled in a series of ambushes, bombardments and battles that not even a succession of sorties by the paratroopers of 8 BPC, 1 BPC, 6 BPC, 1 BEP, 5 BPVN, 2/1 RCP and elements of 3 BT north and north-east from Dien Bien Phu could alleviate. Some of these sorties were conducted by multiple battalions, these groups being commanded by GAP 1 or GAP 2. But nothing could prevent the disaster that had begun with the final evacuation of Lai Chau on 10 December. With crippling casualties, wholesale desertions, and the terror and utter chaos of almost two weeks of continuous combat, between 10 and 22 December almost 2,000 T'ai soldiers, two French officers, fourteen French sergeants and several hundred T'ai civilian dependants simply disappeared without trace in the vast tract of dense jungle that lay between Lai Chau and Dien Bien Phu. In addition to the human cost to the French Union forces, a regiment's worth of weapons had been lost to the Viet Minh.

The total evacuation of Lai Chau, which removed the French Union's former focus from the T'ai region, and the very evident difficulties involved in operating effectively from Dien Bien Phu into the surrounding hills and jungle, posed serious questions for Generals Navarre and Cogny. On the one hand, the security of northern Laos apparently required a significant permanent French presence in the T'ai region, and almost 2,000 T'ai personnel had just been lost in an operation linked to establishing that focus at Dien Bien Phu in place of Lai Chau. On the other hand, the appropriateness and capability of Dien Bien Phu either to support the sort of patrol activity originally envisaged by Cogny or to become the fortified hedgehog envisaged by Navarre were already both in doubt, based upon the experience of only the first few weeks of Operation 'Castor' and the final tragedy of Operation 'Pollux'.

# FRENCH ORGANISATION AND DEPLOYMENT

At Dien Bien Phu the command and control arrangements for the base were developing into their final form. The initial airborne assault on 20 November had been commanded by GAP 1, relieved the following day by an airborne division command element (EDAP) headed by Brigadier General Jean Gilles. This headquarters in

**Table 5 – MAIN CENTRAL POSITION AND HQ AREA**

| French Unit Military Designation (main units only) | English Title | Location (refer to map on p.63) | Remarks |
|---|---|---|---|
| GONO Groupement Opérationnel Nord-Ouest) | HQ Dien Bien Phu (but literally 'Group of Operational Forces North-West') | Main HQ area | Commanded by Colonel (later Brigadier General) de Castries from early Dec 53. The central position of Dien Bien Phu was based upon the village of Muong Thanh. |
| 71 CCS (71e Compagnie de Commandement et des Services) | 71st Command and HQ Support Company | Main HQ area (Claudine) | HQ staff and support troops for the entire Dien Bien Phu site. |
| | 2nd Company, 822nd Signal Battalion | Main HQ area (Claudine) | |
| | 2nd Company, 823rd Signal Battalion | Main HQ area (Claudine) | |
| | 403rd Postal Detachment | Main HQ area (Claudine) | The military post office address number at Dien Bien Phu was 'No. 74.144'. |
| | 730th Fuel Supply Company, Depot No. 81 | Main HQ area (Claudine) | |
| | Detachment of 3rd Ammunition Supply Company | Main HQ area | |
| | 1st Quartermaster Operational Exploitation Group | Main HQ area (Claudine) | Elements of 3 REI, detachment of Gendarmerie and Garde Républicaine. |
| ACM 29 | 29th Mobile Surgical Detachment | Main HQ area | Supported Dien Bien Phu's principal medical facility, commanded by Major Paul Grauwin MD. The main hospital was originally established with 44 beds, an operating theatre, recovery and X-ray facilities. In Feb, ACM 29 was reinforced by the Vietnamese Army ACM 44, commanded by Lieutenant Gindrey MD. |
| | 44th Vietnamese Mobile Surgical Detachment | Main HQ area | |
| GC 8/GCMA (8e Groupement de Commandos / Groupement de Commandos Mixtes Aéroportés) | 8th Commando Group of Composite Airborne Commando Group | Main HQ area | |
| | Detachment from HQ DOP | Main HQ area | Intelligence staff. |
| | Detachment 6th Section, French Central Intelligence | Main HQ area | Intelligence staff. |
| | Detachment Military Security troops | | Security and counter-intelligence staff. |

turn had been replaced by Colonel Dominique Bastiani's Paratroop Operational Group (GOP – Groupement Opérationnel Parachutiste) once the valley had been secured, and in order to release Brigadier Gilles to resume his primary duties as the commander of French airborne forces in Indo-China. Then, finally, the GOP had been relieved by the GONO (Groupement Opérationnel Nord-Ouest) on 7 December. This was the headquarters that would be responsible for the direct overall command of Dien Bien Phu throughout the remainder of its existence. The first of very many C-47 supply aircraft landed on the refurbished airstrip on 25

Table 5 – MAIN CENTRAL POSITION AND HQ AREA (continued)

| French Unit Military Designation (main units only) | English Title | Location (refer to map on p. 63) | Remarks |
|---|---|---|---|
| GAP 2 (2e Groupement Aéroporté) | HQ Airborne Battlegroup No. 2 | Main HQ area | Command HQ for airborne forces until 24 Mar, when Lt Col Langlais assumed de facto overall control of the active defence of Dien Bien Phu from de Castries. |
| | 342nd Airborne Signal Company | Main HQ area | |
| 9 CCS (9e Compagnie de Commandement et des Services (Légion Étrangère) | 9th Command and Support Company (Foreign Legion) | Main HQ area | |
| 31 BG (31e Bataillon du Génie) | 31st Engineer Battalion | Main HQ area | Battalion HQ element and 1/31 BG arrived late Dec. 31 BG commanded by Major André Sudrat, principal engineer adviser at Dien Bien Phu. |
| 1/31 BG (1er Compagnie du 31e Bataillon du Génie) | 1st Company, 31st Engineer Battalion | Main HQ area | |
| 3/31 BG (3e Compagnie du 31e Bataillon du Génie) | 3rd Company, 31st Engineer Battalion | Main HQ area | Arrived 4 Dec. |
| | 5th Medium Repair Company (Foreign Legion) | Main HQ area | |
| 3/1RCC (3e Escadron, 1er Régiment de Chasseurs à Cheval) | 3rd Squadron, 1st Regiment of Light Cavalry (Armoured) | Area of main position (with squadron HQ sited adjacent to Claudine) | Squadron HQ and two platoons (seven M-24 tanks). This composite squadron was commanded by Captain Yves Hervouët. |
| 1 BEP (1er Bataillon Étranger de Parachutistes) | 1st Foreign Legion Airborne Battalion | Area of main position | Tactical reserve force. |
| 8 BPC (8e Bataillon de Parachutistes de Choc) | 8th Airborne Assault (or 'Shock') Battalion | Area of main position | Tactical reserve force. |
| 1/13 DBLE (1er Bataillon, 13e Demi-Brigade de Légion Étrangère) | 1st Battalion, 13th Half-Brigade, Foreign Legion | Claudine | Commanded by Major Coutant. |
| 3/10 RAC (3e Groupe, 10e Régiment d'Artillerie Coloniale) | 3rd Group, 10th Colonial Artillery Regiment | Claudine | One battery of four 105mm guns. |
| 2/4 RAC (2e Groupe, 4e Régiment d'Artillerie Coloniale) | 2nd Group, 4th Colonial Artillery Regiment | Claudine | Two batteries (eight 105mm guns). Initially commanded by Major Hourcabie, and later by Major Knecht. An artillery group usually comprises three batteries of four guns each, plus command and control and support elements. |
| 11/4/4 RAC (11e Batterie, 4e Groupe, 4e Régiment d'Artillerie Coloniale) | 11th Battery, 4th Group, 4th Colonial Artillery Regiment | Claudine | Four 155mm medium howitzers |

**Table 5 – MAIN CENTRAL POSITION AND HQ AREA** (continued)

| French Unit Military Designation (main units only) | English Title | Location (refer to map on p.63) | Remarks |
|---|---|---|---|
| 1 CEPML (1re Compagnie Étrangère Parachutiste de Mortiers Lourds) | 1st Foreign Legion Airborne Heavy Mortar Company | Claudine | Twelve 120mm mortars. 1 CEPML commander Lieutenant Jacques Molinier was seriously wounded and evacuated on 11 Mar. Due to successive casualties, command of 1 CEPML subsequently passed to Lieutenants Paul Turcy, Erwan Bergot and finally to Jean Singland.[14] |
| GC 1/22 | Fighter Group 1/22 'Saintonge' | Dien Bien Phu main airstrip | F8F Bearcat fighter aircraft. Six F8F fighters were routinely based at Dien Bien Phu. |
|  | Air Force Signals Company No. 21/74 | Dien Bien Phu main airstrip |  |
| 21 GAOA (21e Groupe Aérien d'Observation d'Artillerie) | 21st Aerial Artillery Observation Group | Dien Bien Phu main airstrip | Morane-500 Cricket aircraft. |
| 23 GAOA (23e Groupe Aérien d'Observation d'Artillerie) | 23rd Aerial Artillery Observation Group | Dien Bien Phu main airstrip | Morane-500 Cricket aircraft. |
|  | Airbase Detachment No. 195 | Dien Bien Phu main airstrip |  |

November, and from December 1953 until early March 1954 the almost division-size garrison that was now commanded by Colonel Christian Marie Ferdinand de la Croix de Castries[15] received further large quantities of additional combat units, together with a multiplicity of support units and *matériel*. By 13 March 1954 these headquarters, combat units, support organisations and assets had been allocated and deployed to the nine principal and numerous secondary or subordinate strong-points that together comprised the defences of Dien Bien Phu.

**Table 6 – THE OTHER PRINCIPAL STRONG-POINTS[16]**

| French Unit Military Designation (main units only) | English Title | Location (refer to map on p.63) | Remarks |
|---|---|---|---|
| 5/7 RTA (5e Bataillon, 7e Régiment de Tirailleurs Algériens) | 5th Battalion, 7th Regiment, Algerian Rifles | Gabrielle | Gabrielle was known as Doc Lap by the Viet Minh. |
| 2 CMMLE (2e Compagnie Mixte de Mortiers de Légion Étrangère) | 2nd Foreign Legion Composite Mortar Company | Gabrielle | Eight 120mm mortars and four 81mm mortars. 2 CMMLE was usually attached to and in support of 5 REI. Deployed to Gabrielle 27 Dec. |
| 3 BT (3e Bataillon T'ai) | 3rd T'ai Infantry Battalion | Anne-Marie | Anne-Marie was known as Ban Keo by the Viet Minh. |
| 1 CMMLE (1er Compagnie Mixte de Mortiers de Légion Étrangère) | 1st Foreign Legion Composite Mortar Company | Anne-Marie | Eight 120mm mortars and four 81mm mortars. 1 CMMLE was usually attached to and in support of 3 REI. |
| 3/13 DBLE (3e Bataillon, 13e Demi-Brigade de Légion Étrangère | 3rd Battalion, 13th Half-Brigade, Foreign Legion | Beatrice | Beatrice was known as Him Lam by the Viet Minh. Commanded by Major Paul Pégot. |
| 3/3 RTA (3e Bataillon, 3e Régiment de Tirailleurs Algériens) | 3rd Battalion, 3rd Regiment, Algerian Rifles | Dominique | Commanded by Captain Jean Garandeau. |
| 2/4 RAC (2e Groupe, 4e Régiment d'Artillerie Coloniale) | 2nd Group, 4th Colonial Artillery | Dominique | One battery of four 105mm guns. |

Table 6 – **THE OTHER PRINCIPAL STRONG-POINTS** (continued)

| French Unit Military Designation (main units only) | English Title | Location (refer to map on p.63) | Remarks |
|---|---|---|---|
| FTA-NVN | North Vietnam Anti-Aircraft Artillery Group | Dominique 4 | One section of two M-16 quad-.50cal heavy machine-guns. |
| 1/4 RTM (1er Bataillon, 4e Régiment de Tirailleurs Marocains) | 1st Battalion, 4th Regiment, Moroccan Rifles | Eliane | Commanded by Major Jean Nicholas. The battalion headquarters was based in the concrete cellar of the former residence of the French colonial governor. |
| 2 BT (2e Bataillon T'ai) | 2nd T'ai Infantry Battalion | Eliane | |
| 2/31 BG (2e Compagnie du 31e Bataillon du Génie) | 2nd Company, 31st Engineer Battalion | Eliane 10 | Arrived by 21 Dec. |
| 1/2 REI (1er Bataillon, 2e Régiment Étranger d'Infanterie) | 1st Battalion, 2nd Foreign Legion Infantry Regiment | Huguette | |
| FTA-NVN | North Vietnam Anti-Aircraft Artillery Group | Huguette 1 | One section of two M-16 quad-.50cal heavy machine-guns. |
| GMPT 1 (1er Groupement Mobile de Partisans T'ai) | T'ai Partisan Mobile Group No. 1 | Françoise | Total of eleven companies, but with some detached to other strong-points. |
| 3/3 REI (3e Bataillon, 3e Régiment Étranger d'Infanterie) | 3rd Battalion, 3rd Foreign Legion Infantry Regiment | Isabelle | Isabelle was known as Hong Cum by the Viet Minh. 3/3 REI was commanded by Major Henri Grand d'Esnon. |
| 2/1 RTA (2e Bataillon, 1er Régiment de Tirailleurs Algériens) | 2nd Battalion, 1st Regiment, Algerian Rifles | Isabelle | |
| 3/10 RAC (3e Groupe, 10e Régiment d'Artillerie Coloniale) | 3rd Group, 10th Colonial Artillery Regiment | Isabelle | Two batteries (eight 105mm guns). Commanded by Major Alliou. |
| 3/1RCC (3e Escadron, 1er Régiment de Chasseurs à Cheval) | 3rd Squadron, 1st Regiment, Light Cavalry (Armoured) | Isabelle | One platoon (three M-24 tanks). Commanded by Lieutenant Henri Préaud. |

The potential vulnerability of these widely dispersed strong-points might have been mitigated by the establishment of permanent positions on the heights surrounding the valley, but such action was neither planned nor indeed achievable by the limited French Union forces available.

Between 1 December 1953 and mid-March 1954, the further development of the Dien Bien Phu base proceeded, as it prepared to deal with what was generally regarded as the inevitable attack that General Giap's forces would in due course launch against it. But while the preparation of the emplacements, bunkers and so on continued – though without the benefit of sufficient quantities of defence stores, or suitable local materials to compensate for this – the units of the garrison mounted a series of operations or sorties into the region surrounding the base. A summary (Table 7) of the more significant of these operations illustrates the increasing constraints – on movement beyond the garrison in particular – imposed upon the French by the Viet Minh as the communist

**Table 7 – FRENCH SORTIES AND OPERATIONS, DECEMBER 1953 – MARCH 1954**

| Date(s) | French Unit(s) Involved | Summary of Operation | Remarks |
|---|---|---|---|
| 1–15 Dec 53 | 8 BPC(-) One company 3 BT | Mission to establish contact with local guerrilla units in T'ai mountains to the north and seize control of the important road junction at Tuan Giao 80 kms NE of Dien Bien Phu. Force penetrated about 30 kms into the mountains. Later, this force also attempted, unsuccessfully, to join the GAP 2 operation to save the T'ai garrison at Muong Pon (see below). | |
| 1–5 Dec 53 | 1 BPC 2/1 RCP | Mission to clear Route 41 towards the village of Him Lam and the high ground to the NE. Heavily engaged by Viet Minh Battalion No. 888 of Infantry Regiment No. 176 of the 316th Division less than 5 kms from Dien Bien Phu. French lost 14 dead and 26 wounded. | Led to the decision to establish a position on Hill 506 to secure the approach along Route 41. Hill 506 subsequently (10 Dec) became strong-point Beatrice. |
| 7–10 Dec 53 | GAP 1 (1 BPC and 6 BPC) | Repeated the 1 BPC and 2/1 RCP operation to secure Route 41 to NE. Secured area more than 6 kms beyond Him Lam and enabled subsequent work to develop Beatrice position. Viet Minh attempts to attack this force on 9 Dec were dealt with successfully. | |
| 11–15 Dec 53 | GAP 2 (1 BEP, 5 BPVN and 8 BPC(-)) | Mission to assist the T'ai forces that had withdrawn from Lai Chau after 10 Dec and relieve the T'ai garrison under attack at Muong Pon (part-way to Lai Chau). 8 BPC ambushed and stopped at Ban Tau, and the remainder of GAP 2 were pinned down until the morning of 12 Dec. Advance continued 12 and 13 Dec, arriving 1400 to find garrison overrun with no survivors. GAP 2 began to withdraw at 1530, but was ambushed by the Viet Minh at 1650, who were temporarily forced away by B-26 bomber strikes. Battle resumed between the GAP 2 rearguard, 1 BEP, and advancing Viet Minh forces. Air support finally assisted a break-clean at 1830. Last elements of GAP 2 re-entered Dien Bien Phu at 0735, 15 Dec. GAP 2 casualties during this sortie included about 60 dead and missing, plus 69 wounded. | Involved the remainder of 8 BPC that had not deployed on 1 Dec. |

**Table 7 – FRENCH SORTIES AND OPERATIONS, DECEMBER 1953 – MARCH 1954** (continued)

| Date(s) | French Unit(s) Involved | Summary of Operation | Remarks |
|---|---|---|---|
| 15–21 Dec 53 | 5 BPVN | Mission to secure, prepare and fortify area 3 kms NW of the airstrip, which became strong-point Anne-Marie. | |
| 21–26 Dec 53 | GAP 2 (1 BEP, 8 BPC) | Mission (Operation 'Régate') to link up at Sop Nao the forces from Dien Bien Phu with French Union forces advancing (Operation 'Ardèche') from Laos (since 3 Dec, and opposed much of the way). Linkup at Sop Nao achieved 1200, 23 Dec. | Despite considerable Viet Minh action against Operation 'Ardèche' force, that from Dien Bien Phu sustained only one fatality by enemy action. High profile of link-up provided the French high command with false lessons on the viability of Dien Bien Phu as support base for deep penetration patrol operations. |
| 29 Dec 53 | 3/13 DBLE(-) | Mission to clear road beyond Him Lam (Beatrice) halted by Viet Minh forces. | |
| 30 Dec 53 | 2 BM | Mission to exploit southwards from Isabelle halted by Viet Minh 5 kms south at Ban Cang. | 2 BM, together with 301 BVN, was removed from Dien Bien Phu soon after and was replaced by other troops. |
| 6–8 Jan 54 | 8 BPC | Mission to reconnoitre Route 41 as far as possible towards Tuan Giao. 8 BPC ambushed, but retired in good order. At the village of Na Loi a Viet Minh force blocked the withdrawal. French air force fighter-bombers destroyed the village and 8 BPC returned to Dien Bien Phu at 1200, 8 Jan. | |
| 12 Jan 54 | GAP 2 (complete) | Raid mounted against Huoi Phuc, 3 kms SW of Isabelle. | |
| 31 Jan–2 Feb 54 | GAP 2 (complete), 2 BT and 3/3 REI | Major attack against Viet Minh defensive positions on Hill 683, 2 kms from Gabrielle. This preceded a concerted (but largely unsuccessful) effort by infantry, artillery and air power from 6 Feb 54 to identify and destroy the Viet Minh artillery positions. During this attack the Viet Minh overran a platoon of 2 BT and recovered from the dead platoon commander, Lieutenant Nègre, a large-scale map of the entire French deployment in the valley. | On 31 Jan communist 75mm howitzers and 105mm guns of Artillery Regiment No. 45 first fired on Dominique, Eliane and the airstrip. Incoming aircraft were also fired on by 37mm AA guns of Flak Regiment No. 367. |
| 6–7 Feb 54 | GAP 2 (complete), 2 BT, 1/4 RTM and elements of 31 BG | Mission to attack and destroy Viet Minh positions on Hills 754 to 781, 4 kms west of Dien Bien Phu, which dominated the valley. Force arrived at mountain crest at 1115 unopposed, and found no communist artillery. Then, at 1300, it was suddenly hit by a major attack. At 1820 the force withdrew to Him Lam (Beatrice), arriving 6 hours later. French casualties numbered almost 100. | The Viet Minh artillery was not positioned on the reverse slope in accordance with traditional artillery doctrine, but had been dug into positions on the forward slopes of these hills, and so fired directly on to Dien Bien Phu. |

encirclement of Dien Bien Phu strengthened and tightened with each week that passed.

By 13 March 1954 the garrison had, to the best of its ability, maximised its defensive capability within the significant resource constraints that had been imposed upon it as a result of the decisions that had been taken far away from the maze of bunkers, weapon pits and trenches that now criss-crossed and were dotted about the valley floor. With the fundamental concept of Dien Bien Phu in

Opposite page: A confident Major General Cogny (centre) and Major Bigeard (6 BPC) soon after the initial airborne landings. Brigadier General Gilles is on the left.

**Table 7 – FRENCH SORTIES AND OPERATIONS, DECEMBER 1953 – MARCH 1954** (continued)

| Date(s) | French Unit(s) Involved | Summary of Operation | Remarks |
|---|---|---|---|
| 9 Feb 54 | 1/13 DBLE, 1/2 REI, one company 1/4 RTM, and one T'ai company | Mission to reconnoitre to Hong Lech Cang, 5 kms west of Dien Bien Phu. Engaged at the village by Viet Minh troops wearing captured French camouflage uniforms. French casualties 7 dead, 21 wounded. | |
| 10–15 Feb 54 | GAP 2 (complete), 3/13 DBLE, and one company 5/7 RTA | Mission to clear Hill 674, 1 km east of Gabrielle, stopped by mid-morning by Viet Minh fire from bunkers and entrenched positions. French artillery support dropped short and killed fifteen 5/7 RTA soldiers. Advance resumed 13 Feb, with heavy support by B-26 bombers, when the force captured the Viet Minh positions and destroyed them; at cost of many more casualties. But they were too far away to be held and the force withdrew on 15 Feb. | The Viet Minh had been able to develop strong defensive positions with relative impunity, as the French artillery had insufficient reserves of ammunition to engage them during the period when they were being constructed, at which time they were at their most vulnerable. |
| 11–15 Feb 54 | 3/3 REI and 3/3 RTA(-) | Mission to clear Viet Minh positions that were increasingly closing on and threatening Beatrice. Advance stalled in area Hill 781 at 1315, with heavy casualties due to Viet Minh fire from emplaced positions, and withdrew to Kha Chit, almost 2 kms south of Beatrice. Subsequently withdrew along Route 41, assisted by M-24 tanks of 3/1 RCC. | By 15 Feb the garrison had lost 32 officers, 96 NCOs and 836 enlisted men since 20 Nov 53 (a total of about 10 per cent of the original strength). This total did not include the more than 2,000 casualties incurred by the Operation 'Pollux' force from Lai Chau in Nov 53. |
| 4 Mar 54 | 3 BT and 5/7 RTA | Mission to remove Viet Minh from positions on Hill 633, 1 km north of Gabrielle, stopped by heavy fire and forced to withdraw. | |
| 5 Mar 54 | 1 BEP | Mission to clear Hill 781, which dominated the Route 41 approach to Dien Bien Phu, forced to withdraw in face of heavy fire from well dug-in and camouflaged bunkers and trenches. | |
| 11 Mar 54 | GAP 2 | Mission to clear Viet Minh from Hill 555, which overlooked Beatrice and was also just 3 kms from the main command post at Dien Bien Phu. Attack stalled and GAP 2 withdrew at 1700 that afternoon. | By 11 Mar the French Union forces at Dien Bien Phu had comprehensively lost control of all the high ground that dominated every one of their positions. |

mind, a brief review of the artillery, combat air, engineer and armour capabilities is instructive. First, however, it is necessary to outline the general organisation and composition of the infantry units that had already been engaged in regular combat since 20 November 1953, and were shortly destined to carry out most of the bitter fighting to defend Dien Bien Phu against the main Viet Minh assault.

# COMBAT CAPABILITY OF THE FRENCH UNION FORCES

## Infantry

The organisation and equipment of the infantry units at Dien Bien Phu varied in matters of detail between regiments and battalions and a detailed description of each unit is beyond the scope of this account. Suffice it to say that a French infantry regiment was usually based upon a three-battalion organisation, and each battalion usually comprised three – but often four and sometimes more – rifle companies plus a headquarters and support company, within which were the battalion's support or 'heavy' weapons. Typically, by 1953, airborne battalions had four rifle companies. A battalion might number anything between 400 and 1,000 personnel, although the strength of the infantry battalions at Dien Bien Phu averaged about 600–700 soldiers as at mid-March 1954. In addition to a variety of French, US and British small-arms and equipment, the battalion usually had numbers of recoilless rifles in 57mm or 75mm calibre, plus 60mm and 81mm mortars (usually four of the latter per battalion), and .30cal medium machine-guns. These support weapons were grouped in sections within the support company, and were also found within the headquarters platoons of some battalions, including those of the airborne units. The headquarters element of the infantry battalion fulfilled the command and support functions of administration, communications, transport and medical. From 1953, a number of independent heavy mortar companies, equipped with 120mm mortars or a mix of 120mm and 81mm mortars, were formed to provide additional support for infantry units. The general appearance of French infantry units in combat was almost identical with that of US army units of the late 1940s, much of the camouflage clothing invariably worn by the airborne units being of US or British origin, while the use of US or British web equipment and the ubiquitous US M-1 helmet was virtually universal throughout the French Union forces. Non-paratroop units wore plain olive drab French-pattern combat clothing, although much of this was procured in Indo-China. Only the troops' parade dress, rank insignia and soft headdress (beret, képi, chéchia, side-cap) provide clear evidence of their French nationality, origins or affiliation.

In 1954 the French Union infantry units at Dien Bien Phu fell into various categories. First, there were the airborne or parachute units: the paratroops. The airborne units were further categorised as metropolitan (2/1 RCP, 8 BPC), colonial (1 BPC, 6 BPC), Foreign Legion (1 BEP, 2 BEP, 1 CEPML), or non-European (5 BPVN). The airborne battalions included large numbers of locally recruited soldiers, so that typically up to 50 per cent of their manpower was Vietnamese by 1954, with an authorised establishment of 446 Europeans and 406 Vietnamese. The fighting quality of these Vietnamese paratroopers was generally of a high order. Although the overall nature of the operation and preponderance of airborne units at Dien Bien Phu has sometimes created an impression that it was a battle fought exclusively by these élite paratroop units, there were also several non-airborne infantry units in the garrison; many of which later gave very good accounts of themselves during the main battle.

Once again, these infantry units fell into the same sub-categories. There were no non-airborne metropolitan or colonial infantry battalions at Dien Bien Phu, but the Foreign Legion units and independent mortar companies included 1/2 REI, 3/3 REI, 1/13 DBLE, 3/13 DBLE, 1 CMMLE and 2 CMMLE. But those accounts of Dien Bien Phu which have over-emphasised the albeit considerable Foreign Legion contribution to the battle do also need to be balanced by an understanding of the fact that the involvement of French Union units recruited from North Africa and in Indo-China itself was also extensive. The non-European infantry included T'ai units (2 BT, 3 BT), Algerians (2/1 RTA, 5/7 RTA, 3/3 RTA), Moroccans (1/4 RTM), and T'ai partisans (GMPT 1). The Moroccan 2 BM and Vietnamese 301 BVN also served briefly at Dien Bien Phu, but had been withdrawn by mid-March 1954. Indeed, a statistical summary of the ethnic mix of the whole garrison of Dien Bien Phu in the period mid-March to the beginning of May 1954 showed quite starkly the extent to which French colonial policies and ambitions were to a considerable extent being defended by non-Frenchmen and by the soldiers of the Foreign Legion, see table 8.

Inevitably, the infantry was the most numerous combat arm overall and it bore the brunt of the fighting. But throughout the life of Dien Bien Phu, the infantry had always understood and believed that, once battle was finally joined, the French artillery would ensure that the Viet Minh would never be able to reach the relatively lightly constructed bunkers in which they lived – far less to overwhelm the fairly *ad hoc* defences that they manned. In that belief they would prove to be sadly disillusioned.

**Artillery**

The artillery commander at Dien Bien Phu was Colonel Charles Piroth, who was also the deputy commander to Colonel de Castries. Piroth was forty-

### Table 8 – COMPOSITION OF FRENCH UNION GARRISON

| Ethnic or National Category | Officers | Non-Commissioned Officers | Enlisted Personnel | Totals |
|---|---|---|---|---|
| French Metropolitan | 272 | 780 | 1758 | 2810 |
| Foreign Legion | 128 | 440 | 3363 | 3931 |
| North African | 2 | 168 | 2467 | 2637 |
| African | — | 8 | 239 | 247 |
| Vietnamese* | 11 | 270 | 5199 | 5480 |
| **Totals** | **413** | **1,666** | **13,026** | **15,105** |

* Regular and Auxiliary Personnel (including 2,575 T'ai personnel)

### Table 9 – SUMMARY OF FRENCH UNION ARTILLERY AT DIEN BIEN PHU

| Category | Quantity | Remarks |
|---|---|---|
| 105mm field guns | 24 | With 27,400 rounds available on 13 Mar 54. Direct fire weapons such as recoilless rifles and mortars were also available within the heavy weapons platoons of infantry units. |
| 120mm heavy mortars | 28 | With 22,000 rounds available on 13 Mar 54. In addition to the heavy mortars, 81mm mortars were available within the heavy weapons platoons of infantry battalions and the two Foreign Legion composite mortar companies. Uniquely, 1 CEPML had twelve 120mm mortars. |
| 155mm medium howitzers | 4 | With 2,700 rounds available on 13 Mar 54. Primary role of these guns was counter-battery tasks. |
| .50cal heavy machine-guns (quad-mounted) | 4 | Two sections, each of two 4-barrelled, electrically powered, anti-aircraft gun systems, mounted on M-16 half-track vehicles. Commanded by Lieutenant Redon. |

eight, an experienced artilleryman, who had lost his left arm during the fighting in Italy in 1943. He was described as a jovial and sensitive man, and subsequent events would indicate that perhaps over-optimistic or over-confident might have been added to this description. Certainly he was convinced of the efficacy of the artillery under his command and of its absolute superiority over any artillery that the Viet Minh might, possibly, manage to deploy against Dien Bien Phu. His combat experience in Indo-China included command of the 69th North African Artillery Regiment and he had taken command of the artillery support organisation at Dien Bien Phu on 7 December, subsequently overseeing the steady build-up of artillery assets that commenced on that day. As at 13 March the French Union troops had available a considerable quantity of artillery. This reflected the high command's belief that the success – and survival – of the base would depend ultimately upon the effectiveness of its counter-battery fire and its ability to destroy the massed infantry attacks by the Viet Minh that were anticipated, based upon past experience of communist tactics (most recently those used by the Chinese in the Korean War). But, given that the Dien Bien Phu garrison equated roughly to a division-size formation, its artillery was still some three batteries of 105mm guns and two batteries of 155mm guns short of the fire support that its commander might reasonably have expected.

In addition to a multiplicity of medium (81mm) and light (60mm) mortars, 57mm and 75m recoilless rifles and medium machine-guns that were integral to the various combat units at Dien Bien Phu, the garrison was supported by two artillery groups, each of three 105mm batteries. In addition, there was one battery of 155mm howitzers, and three companies equipped with heavy (120mm) mortars. The artillery was grouped into Groupement A (3/10 RAC plus two 120mm mortar companies) and Groupement B (2/4 RAC plus 11/4/4 RAC, one 120mm mortar company and the sections of quad-.50cal heavy machine-guns).

For the French Union forces and the Viet Minh alike, the US M2 (or M101) 105mm howitzer was the principal field artillery weapon employed at Dien Bien Phu, see table 10.

From the outset the French artillery plan was fatally flawed, depending as it did upon the fire of the Dien Bien Phu guns being observed and adjusted from observation posts on the high ground adjacent to the main positions and by observers in the six Morane-500 Cricket aircraft that were based at Dien Bien Phu. The faith displayed in the use of air-power to support the artillery mirrored the original wider planning assumption that French combat and supply aircraft would enjoy unrestricted access to the skies above the valley at all times. This assumption was extraordinary, and underlines the unshakeable over-optimism of the high command with regard to the overall capability of its forces.

By mid-March the increasingly less successful sorties, and ever tightening circle of Viet Minh positions about Dien Bien Phu meant that no observation posts could be placed on the on the high ground, and it was immediately obvious that the consequent reliance upon aerial artillery observation meant that the artillery

Table 10 – SPECIFICATIONS OF THE M2 (M101) AND M101A1 HOWITZER

| Category | Specification | Remarks |
|---|---|---|
| Official Designations | M2 Howitzer | Entered US Army service as the M2 howitzer in 1939. |
| | M101 Howitzer (M2A1 gun carriage) | Later the M2 was re-designated M101, then M101A1 (which had a modified gun carriage). |
| | M101A1 Howitzer (M2A2 gun carriage) | Production of the M101A1 ended in 1953, by which date 10,202 M2 (M101) and M101A1 guns had been made. |
| Calibre | 105mm | Barrel life about 20,000 rounds |
| Crew | 8 | |
| Weight | 2,258kg (M101A1) | |
| Length (travelling) | 6 metres (M101A1) | Gun had a split trail design, and was usually towed by a 2.5ton truck. |
| Width (travelling) | 2.2 metres (M101A1) | Including the gun shield to protect the crew from small-arms fire and shell splinters. |
| Ground Clearance | 0.4 metres (M101A1) | |
| Elevation | −4.5° − +66° | |
| Traverse | 23° left and right | |
| Maximum Planning Range | 11,000 metres | |
| Ammunition | High-explosive (HE), high-explosive anti-tank (HEAT), smoke, white phosphorous (WP), chemical, illuminating, leaflet, anti-personnel. | Ammunition types were those in US Army and USMC service in 1954. The ammunition types used at Dien Bien Phu were primarily HE, WP, illuminating and smoke. For planning purposes, the maximum rate of fire was 8rpm for 30 seconds, or 3rpm over an extended period. |

capability and accuracy were totally dependent upon suitable flying weather. But even that dependence became a secondary consideration once the Viet Minh artillery demonstrated its ability to destroy the French aircraft both on the ground and in the air with relative impunity. By 13 March the effectiveness of French counter-battery fire had been severely degraded by this drastically reduced observation capability and, in the aftermath of events that took place shortly afterwards, would soon be reduced to virtually zero; although by then the overwhelming priority was to fire the close-support missions which had generally overtaken the counter-battery task.

Finally, the ever-decreasing number of supply flights into Dien Bien Phu, together with reduced allocations of ammunition as a consequence of having to support the concurrent operations in Laos, the Red River area, and central and southern Vietnam, meant that the garrison never achieved the reserve stocks of ammunition needed to counter the forces that were ranged about them by mid-March. Even if it had acquired such stocks, it is doubtful that it could have stored and protected the ammunition adequately, in light of the paucity of engineer stores available and consequently the limited extent of field engineering work that it could carry out.

**Combat Air Support**

Surprisingly perhaps, given the nature of the base, the whole question of combat air support for Dien Bien Phu can be considered relatively briefly. In essence, it had been envisaged that the thirty bombers, thirty-two fighters and forty-five fighter-bombers flying from their airbases at Hanoi or elsewhere, or from the carrier *Arromanches* and later from the *Bois Belleau*, would interdict any communist forces moving towards the valley and so prevent their build-up. It was also assumed that in the most unlikely event of any shortfall of French artillery fire-power such a capability gap would be more than compensated for by the use of air-power.

While denial of the Dien Bien Phu airstrips to all but the half-dozen F8F Bearcats that it had intended would be based there throughout was not critical for these aircraft, other unforeseen factors certainly were. The frequently poor flying weather combined with the success of the communist camouflage to constrain air operations and make effective target acquisition and engagement virtually impossible. The communists also conducted their offensive operations by night wherever possible, secure in the knowledge that the French air force ground-attack and precision bombing capabilities at night were extremely limited. But the greatest surprise for the French pilots was undoubtedly the sheer scale and devastating effect of the communist anti-aircraft fire, both at Dien Bien Phu and along the various Viet Minh supply routes. In November forty-five aircraft sustained hits, three being shot down, and the following month forty-nine were hit. Between January and May 1954, anti-aircraft fire destroyed sixty-two aircraft, and 167 were badly damaged.

The French air force concentrated initially on trying to cut the communist logistics line of communication along and linked to Route 41. But the Viet Minh proved adept at repairing damaged roads and buildings while concealing brand-new ones, so that all attempts to halt the flow of *matériel* – other than very temporarily – failed. The pilots of the F8F Bearcats, SB-2C Helldivers, F6F Hellcats and eighteen F4U Corsairs of the two fighter and three carrier-based flotillas, and of the B-26 Marauders and PB4Y2 Privateers of the one bomber group and one bomber flotilla, flew their missions in often appalling weather, in the face of heavy anti-aircraft fire and at enormous personal risk. Although the napalm drops, machine-gun strafing and bombing attacks undoubtedly caused very many casualties to the Viet Minh military units and the endless columns of heavily laden porters on the ground, the French air force, largely for reasons beyond its control (though these should have been anticipated) was unable to prevent the Viet Minh achieving a viable offensive capability at Dien Bien Phu. Neither was it able to provide the sort of close air support so desperately needed by the garrison once its own artillery had been neutralised and the main communist assault was under way.

**Engineer Support**

Initially, the probable role of Dien Bien Phu as perceived by Major General Cogny (and therefore by the original Operation 'Castor' airborne commanders Gilles, Langlais and Bigeard) had resulted in minimal work being carried out to construct defences beyond basic trenches and weapon pits, and to improve the airstrip sufficiently to support the landing and take-off of re-supply flights. The early work had been carried out by the 17 CGP, but from 4 December the arrival at the airstrip of the first elements of 31 BG heralded the start of more substantial construction work. The mission that had been given to Major André Sudrat, the commander of 31 BG, was not merely formidable, it was impossible. As well as providing the principal fortifications for Dien Bien Phu, all of which had to be sufficiently robust to withstand 105mm artillery shells, 31 BG was required to build two Bailey bridges capable of bearing the movement across them of light tanks, to provide electric light and power for the garrison (which was supported by fifteen generators and five battery chargers), to process and purify (using four water purifiers) the daily supply of drinking water for more than 10,000 men, to upgrade the airstrip at the main position, and finally to build a new airstrip adjacent to strong-point Isabelle to the south. Later, the engineers would also be required to address the implications for Dien Bien Phu of widespread flooding when the monsoon rains arrived.

To complete the fortifications for the garrison would have required at least 36,000 tons of defence stores. Although some 2,200 tons of wood and other materials were acquired from the surrounding area, the shortfall of almost 34,000 tons was equivalent to about 12,000 transport aircraft cargo loads. Based on the norm of eighty supply flights per day, and if nothing but defence stores and engineer equipment had been flown to Dien Bien Phu, five months' worth of re-supply flights would have been needed to make Dien Bien Phu a viable defensive position; an entirely unrealistic proposition. In practice, the actual allocation of combat engineer resources made by the staff for Dien Bien Phu amounted to no more than 4,000 tons and these were sub-allocated as in table 11.

Consequently, throughout the life of Dien Bien Phu there was a permanent shortfall of some 30,000 tons of the basic stores and equipment that were absolutely vital to the successful conduct of what was patently about to develop into a major defensive battle. The lack of these essential resources, and the fact that the quantity allocated fell so far short of that required, was one of the most important factors that contributed directly to the early destruction of many of the garrison's key weapons and assets by the communist artillery, and to the high casualties sustained by units whose positions had either insufficiently robust overhead protection to withstand shells and mortar bombs, or no overhead protection whatsoever. The task of the Viet Minh artillery observers was further assisted by the failure of the garrison to camouflage or conceal their principal command and control (all too evident from their forests of radio antennae) and artillery positions, another task to which a properly resourced engineer unit could have made a major contribution if

**Table 11 – ENGINEER RESOURCES**

| Tonnage Allocated | Resource Category |
|---|---|
| 44 | Bailey bridge sections, sufficient to construct two bridges. |
| 70 | Five bulldozers. |
| 510 | Pierced steel plates (PSP) for airstrip construction. |
| 118.5 | Timber beams for bunker construction and overhead protection for trenches. |
| 3,000 | Barbed wire, pickets and associated materials. |
| 23 | Mines and explosives (M & E). |

there had been time. The failure adequately to support the engineer plan at Dien Bien Phu was symptomatic of the early high-level ambiguity surrounding the future role of the position, as well as the extent to which the resources of the French Union forces in Indo-China had become severely overstretched by late 1953. It also indicates yet again the complacency of the high command concerning the ability of the Viet Minh to inflict significant damage upon the French forces in open battle.

**Armour**

It would have been strange perhaps if Colonel de Castries – the flamboyant cavalryman – had not had some armour under his command at Dien Bien Phu, and indeed during December he had a composite squadron – the 3/1 RCC – of ten unassembled M-24 Chaffee light tanks airlifted into the garrison. There the 18-ton US tanks were reassembled by hand, without benefit of anything remotely resembling the factory production line on which they had originally been produced. The reconstruction was conducted in an environment beset by clouds of fine sand that infiltrated all the components, and necessitated their constant cleaning and re-cleaning. The work was carried out by the 2nd Automobile Repair Company of the 5 REI (2/5 CRALE), commanded by Lieutenant Bugeat. At the conclusion of the first phase of this remarkable engineering feat, on 25 December 1953, the first platoon of three tanks was declared operational. Thereafter one more tank was put together every two days, and by 17 January 3/1 RCC was fully operational, under the command of Captain Yves Hervouët. On 1 February, tanks of the squadron were first used in action, in the area north-east of strong-point Gabrielle. Although production of the M-24 dated back to the final year of the Second World War, and its light construction made it vulnerable to post-1945 tanks and anti-armour weapons, it was well-suited for counter-insurgency missions. In the 1950s the M-24 Chaffee light tank was widely used by many Third World armed forces together with those of several European nations including France.

Although some re-allocation of the ten tanks took place later as the battle progressed and casualties occurred – several disabled M-24s subsequently serving as static strong-points – the

**Table 12 – M-24 CHAFFEE LIGHT TANK – GENERAL SPECIFICATIONS**

| Category | Specification |
|---|---|
| Armament | One M-6 75mm gun, elevation −10° − +15°. |
| | One .30 co-axial MMG. |
| | One .30 front hull MMG. |
| | One .50 HMG (mounted at commander's hatch). |
| Ammunition Carried | 48 rounds 75mm. |
| | 3,750 rounds .30 MMG. |
| | 440 rounds .50 HMG. |
| Crew | 4 (but could carry 5). |
| Length | 5.4 metres. |
| Width | 2.70 metres. |
| Height | 2.70 metres (to top of turret HMG); 2.40 metres (to top of turret). |
| Weight | 18 tons. |
| Range | 180 kilometres. |
| Speed (maximum) | 55kph. |
| Armour | 10-38mm. |
| Fording | 1.05 metres. |
| Fuel | Petrol (tank capacity 110 US gallons). |
| Engine | Two Cadillac model 44T24 V8, developing 110bhp at 3,400rpm. |

**Table 13 – DEPLOYMENT OF 3/1 RCC**

| Sub-Unit | Location | Commander (on deployment) | Tanks Allocated (showing names allocated to individual tanks) |
|---|---|---|---|
| Squadron HQ | Main position | Captain Yves Hervouët | One M-24: 'Bazeilles'. |
| 1st Platoon | Main position | Sergent-Chef Aristide Carette | Three M-24s: 'Conti', 'Douamont', 'Ettlingen'. |
| 2nd Platoon | Main position | Sergent Guntz | Three M-24s: 'Auerstadt', 'Posen', 'Smolensk'. |
| 3rd Platoon | Isabelle | Lieutenant Henri Préaud | Three M-24s: 'Ratisbonne', 'Neumach', 'Mulhouse'. |

three tank platoons were initially deployed as per table 13.

Throughout the life of Dien Bien Phu the primary role of the composite squadron – whether employed as sub-units or (as eventually became the case) as individual tanks – was to support counter-attacks by (usually) the paratroop battalions that were held as a tactical reserve. The two sections of American M-16 quad-.50cal heavy machine-guns mounted on half-track vehicles provided additional mobile fire-power to complement the operations carried out by the M-24s. The impact of the 3/1 RCC squadron at Dien Bien Phu was considerable, and had the composite squadron been established at its full strength of seventeen tanks, or had a second squadron been allocated to Dien Bien Phu, it is likely that this highly mobile direct fire support would have had a dramatic effect upon the outcome of the expeditionary probes of January and February. Viet Minh bunkers and trenches on forward slopes could have been acquired and engaged accurately at short range with weapons protected by the M-24s' armour. Surprisingly perhaps, given the cavalry origins of Colonel de Castries, the combat potential of armour at Dien Bien Phu was not exploited as fully as it might have been, the overall lack of tanks and the separation of strong-point Isabelle from the main position resulted in their use piecemeal, with the consequent dissipation of the combat power and shock action that the squadron might have achieved if it had been employed as a single entity.

Although the failure and vulnerability of the French artillery has routinely been cited as the principal weakness of Dien Bien Phu, the shortfall in engineering capability was almost certainly the critical factor which from the outset ensured the ultimate fate of the position, and the blame for failing to assess correctly or provide the necessary engineer resources in December must lie firmly with the staff planners and commanders in Saigon and Hanoi. Meanwhile, the failure to expand significantly and capitalise upon the mobile fire-power, offensive action and counter-attack capability provided by the tanks in the valley also denied the garrison the chance to compensate for the lack of physical protection that might otherwise have been provided by adequate field defences, and for the inability of the artillery to forestall the Viet Minh attack plans. Finally, even without the benefit of adequate artillery and engineer support, a force of (say) about thirty tanks operating against infantry unsupported by armour might well have been able to pre-empt, halt – or possibly even defeat – the main Viet Minh assault that was eventually launched against Dien Bien Phu. But well before the assault General Giap had ensured that the inherent weaknesses of the French Union forces and their positions had been rigorously identified and tested in anticipation of their later exploitation by the communist forces.

# COMBAT CAPABILITY OF THE COMMUNIST FORCES

## Giap's Assessment and Plan

While the French troops had been busy developing their positions, the Viet Minh had been anything but idle. From the outset, in December, General Vo Nguyen Giap had assessed correctly General Navarre's perception of the role of Dien Bien Phu.[17] He had also identified what he termed Navarre's 'arrogance' in challenging the communists to attack what the French commander-in-chief had come to believe was 'an impregnable fortress'. Giap knew that the defences were flawed – tactically and logistically – and, having decided to attack the base, he developed a straightforward concept of operations for the coming confrontation. He knew that 'to ensure victory it was necessary to have a three-to-one superiority of manpower and a five-to-one superiority of fire-power' and understood that 'after the opening of the first breach one must immediately penetrate into the interior of the enemy fortified system and hold that penetration to the bitter end'. Giap appreciated that the isolated garrison's existence depended absolutely upon the two airstrips that supported it: primarily the one close to Muong Thanh, about which village lay the main strength of the French Union forces. He also knew that the best of Navarre's troops had been deployed to Dien Bien Phu. From this assessment he deduced that time would be needed to position his own divisions in order to achieve the superiority of forces and fire-power he needed. Furthermore, he knew that before

Below: A column of Viet Minh infantry marching to reinforce the communist forces at Dien Bien Phu.

any major direct assault could be launched the Viet Minh would have to neutralise the airstrips so as to deny the French any air-landing capability. But he also knew – from earlier bitter experience – that specific anti-aircraft measures would be needed to deal with the French artillery observation aircraft, and with the fighters and bombers that could support the garrison without need of the airstrips. Finally, Giap understood very well that if he could destroy the élite French Union units that garrisoned Dien Bien Phu – the paratroop battalions and Foreign Legionnaires in particular – he would have improved very significantly the communists' operational situation throughout Vietnam. Consequently, he was clear that the operation should attract the highest priority, all other Viet Minh campaigns being relegated (if necessary) to a secondary or holding role until the battle of Dien Bien Phu was concluded. With a view to satisfying these fundamental principles, General Giap set about preparing and positioning his forces for the impending battle.

**Organisation and Force Development**

By mid-March 1954, the communist forces surrounding the Dien Bien Phu valley numbered some 37,500 combat troops, with a further 10,000 held in reserve. The overall strength in the valley area was about 79,000, including service support troops. This force level reflected the high priority Giap had accorded the operation, although it was still but a part of the total of 125,000 regular personnel that were under his control as at late 1953. In addition, throughout the whole of Vietnam, the communist forces also included some 75,000 regional and 250,000 popular force personnel.

Between December 1953 and mid-March 1954, all but one of the regular divisions of the PAVN concentrated in the Dien Bien Phu area, together with a number of specialist and independent units and support organisations, see table 14.

The organisation of the PAVN had continued to evolve and change since its birth in 1949. By 1953 the typical division-level command and control organisation of an infantry division usually comprised a headquarters company, communications company, engineer company and political company. Subordinated to this were up to three infantry regiments, each comprising a regimental headquarters platoon, three infantry battalions and one artillery battalion. A medium mortar company was sometimes substituted for the artillery support unit. The normal personnel strength of the division was about 10,000, that of a battalion about 800. The division could be reinforced for a specific operation or campaign by the inclusion in whole or part of one or more of fifteen regionally deployed independent regiments.

The army also included one heavy division, the 351st, which was headed by the usual headquarters, communications and political companies, but with the engineer company replaced by an anti-aircraft artillery battalion. This heavy division had within it two artillery regiments, one medium mortar regiment, an anti-aircraft regiment and one engineer regiment.

Having compared the Chinese PLA and Soviet military systems, Giap chose to rely heavily on Chinese expertise to fill any gaps in his own knowledge and experience, particularly where formation-level operations were concerned. In general, the Viet Minh structured the embryo PAVN on the PLA model. At an early stage General Lo Kuei-po became the chief Chinese military adviser to the Viet Minh high command, and Chinese Generals Chiang Yun-I and Ch'en Keng arrived as additional advisers in August 1950. Indeed, all five of the principal Viet Minh military leaders in the early 1950s had either trained at the PLA's Whampoa Military Academy or had experienced active service with Chinese communist guerrilla units.

**Table 14 – SUMMARY OF THE BUILD-UP OF COMMUNIST FORCES AT DIEN BIEN PHU, NOVEMBER 1953 TO MARCH 1954**

| Unit Title | Commander | Strength and Principal Equipment Types | Remarks |
|---|---|---|---|
| Area (or Army-level) Headquarters | General Vo Nguyen Giap | | Principal Staff Officers: General Wei Guo-quing General (PRC) Li Cheng-hu Chief of Staff: General Hoang Van Thai. |
| Independent Regiment No. 148 | | About 3,000 men | Elements training in Dien Bien Phu valley 20 Nov 53 contested the Operation 'Castor' LZs 20–23 Nov 53 until withdrawn. |
| Infantry Regiment No. 57 (304th Infantry Division) | Colonel Hoang Khai Tien | About 3,000 men | Arrived Dien Bien Phu 24 Jan 54. |
| 308th Infantry Division (the Iron Division) | Major General Vuong Than Vu | About 10,000 men | Arrived Dien Bien Phu Dec 53, continued to Luang Prabang and returned Dien Bien Phu end Jan 54. Included the PAVN's elite 'Capital' Infantry Regiment No. 102, commanded by Lieutenant Colonel Vu Yen. |
| Artillery Regiment No. 675 (308th Infantry Division) | | 24 x 75mm pack howitzers 20 x 120mm mortars | Arrived Dien Bien Phu mid-Dec 53. |
| Artillery Regiment No. 45 | | 36 x 105mm field guns | Arrived Dien Bien Phu early Jan 54. |
| Air Defence Artillery Regiment No. 367 | | 36 x 37mm light anti-aircraft guns (Soviet origin) .50cal heavy machine guns | Arrived Dien Bien Phu 11 Feb 54. |
| Artillery Regiment No. 237 | | 120mm mortars | Arrived Dien Bien Phu late Jan or during Feb 54. |
| Field Rocket Unit | | Twelve Katyusha (Soviet) multiple rocket-launchers (MRL) | Probably under the direct command of army-level artillery staff. |
| 316th Infantry Division | Major General Le Quang Ba | About 10,000 men | Arrived Dien Bien Phu mid-Dec 53. |
| Artillery Battalion No. 980 (316th Infantry Division) | | | Arrived Dien Bien Phu mid-Dec 53. |
| 325th Infantry Division (the 'Golden Star' Division) | | About 10,000 men | Remained in Mekong Delta area of Cochin China to distract and occupy French Union troops that might otherwise have been deployed to Tonkin and Dien Bien Phu. |
| 312th Infantry Division | Major General Le Trong Tan | About 10,000 men | |
| 351st Heavy Division | Major General Vu Hien | 75mm howitzers 48 x 105mm field guns | 105mm guns acquired in 1953 from stocks captured by the PLA from US forces in Korea. |

### Artillery Support

In accordance with his assessment of the need to achieve a five-to-one superiority in artillery, Giap concentrated well over 200 guns, recoilless rifles and rocket-launchers of 75 millimetres or greater calibre in the hills about Dien Bien Phu prior to the main battle. This compared with less than sixty French artillery guns and heavy mortars – a number that was in any case rapidly reduced by the accuracy of the Viet Minh artillery fire once battle was joined. In line with his operational assessment Giap also acquired the services of thirty-six Russian anti-aircraft guns to counter the threat of air bombardment that had caused the Viet Minh considerable numbers of casualties during the earlier years of the war.

### Logistic Support

Clearly this very sizeable force required a substantial amount of logistic support to sustain it, and in many ways, just as the lack of engineer resources in large part sealed the fate of the French at Dien Bien Phu, so the success of the communist logistic supply system virtually guaranteed the final Viet Minh victory. More than 300,000 personnel were involved directly in the business of supplying and supporting the Viet Minh at Dien Bien Phu. Of these, about 50,000 were regular troops of the supply units, who used – whether voluntarily or as impressed labour – more than 200,000 civilians to move *matériel* along the main line of communication, from the Chinese border south to the Red River area. From there, the ammunition, fuel, food and a hundred other categories of essential supplies were moved to the Dien Bien Phu valley along the same Route 41 that featured prominently in the succession of largely abortive French garrison sorties launched towards the north-east.

### Preliminaries

Giap was under no delusions concerning the enormity of the logistic task and the related preparations for the battle that he had set the PAVN. He identified five distinct (although two related specifically to the artillery) activities that reflected the differing terrain and operational needs of his

**Table 15 – SUMMARY OF VIET MINH ARTILLERY AT DIEN BIEN PHU**

| Category | Quantity | Remarks |
|---|---|---|
| 75mm pack howitzers | 48 | Contributed to about 100,000 shells fired into Dien Bien Phu during the battle. |
| 105mm field guns | 48 | Fired about 30,000 shells into Dien Bien Phu during the battle. Subsequently, additional 105mm guns were provided by the PRC to replace battle losses and increase the total number of these weapons available to the Viet Minh. |
| 120mm heavy mortars | 48 | Subsequently, additional heavy mortars were provided by the PRC to replace battle losses and increase the total number of these weapons available to the Viet Minh. |
| 75mm recoilless rifles | 60 | Contributed to about 100,000 shells fired into Dien Bien Phu during the battle. |
| Katyusha multiple rocket-launchers (MRL) | 12 | The precise number, type and specification of these MRLs vary quite considerably between accounts of Dien Bien Phu; but they were most probably the Soviet BM-13 MRL (with sixteen 132mm rockets per launcher) of the Second World War period. The BM-13 MRL was also in service with the Chinese PLA in 1954.[18] The MRLs were first used against the French garrison on 6 May 54 |
| 37mm light anti-aircraft guns | 36 | Protected by a dedicated battalion of infantry. By about late April the overall number of 37mm guns may have been increased by as many as 67, with the addition of a Chinese PLA regular anti-aircraft regiment to the Viet Minh forces (which was requested on about 5 April, following significant Viet Minh losses to air strikes at the conclusion of the battle for Huguette 6). |

forces to achieve the necessary offensive capability, as well as the crucial role that the communist artillery would play in the battle.

**Table 16 – GIAP'S PRE-REQUISITES FOR VICTORY**

| Task | Activities | Remarks |
|---|---|---|
| Mobility | Transform 100 kms of mule track into a vehicle-capable road. | The mule track traversed very hilly country, and almost 100 streams and rivers. |
| | Build more than 12 vehicle bridges. | All bridges had to be viable by about mid-Jan 54 at latest. |
| | Maintain open some 500 kms of route for constant vehicle passage, in spite of flooding, and French air and ground counter-action. | The PAVN vehicle fleet included about 200 former US Army trucks captured in Korea, and 600 Russian 2.5ton Molotava vehicles. All these trucks were supplied to the Viet Minh by the PRC. |
| Artillery deployment | Concentrate and conceal the guns at Dien Bien Phu. | Guns were towed by trucks, grouped together, then camouflaged pending final deployment. |
| | Position the artillery in the hills over a 7 day period. | Guns were moved, mainly by hand, into pre-reconnoitred and prepared positions. Some had to be disassembled and re-assembled once in their final positions. |
| | Provide continuous mobility for the artillery, by building and concealing 5 roads about the valley. | Often constructed where not even a track had existed before. These roads were repaired – usually by night – wherever and whenever necessary. |
| Artillery protection | Construct gun positions capable of withstanding direct hits on the front of the gun emplacement by shells up to 155mm calibre. | Gun positions – most of which were on forward slopes – were carved into solid rock, with many excavated from the rear of the hill or mountain. In addition, camouflage and dummy gun positions were used to deceive the French and cause them to dissipate their stocks of artillery ammunition. |
| Command and control | Construct command posts and communications positions capable of withstanding direct hits on the top of the emplacements by shells up to 155mm calibre. | |
| Logistic support | Provide adequate amounts of ammunition, food and medical supplies to support a 6-month campaign, including a series of high-tempo offensives. | The truck convoys mainly moved by night, running without lights, or used the cover of bad (non-flying) weather. In addition, tens of thousands of converted bicycles, wheelbarrows, donkeys, horses and river craft were used to convey *matériel* along the lines of communication. During the campaign about 2,250 tons of food (including 1,700 tons of rice), 4,500 tons of petrol and up to 1,700 tons of ammunition were moved to the PAVN units at Dien Bien Phu. |

By the night of Friday, 12 March 1954, General Vo Nguyen Giap was satisfied that his forces had contained the French garrison and also achieved the overall capability necessary to overcome the French Union position at Dien Bien Phu. In spite of this, the Viet Minh victory would prove to be neither easy nor early in coming. Indeed, despite the numerical superiority of the communists, there were points during the forthcoming battle when its outcome was possibly less certain than Giap no doubt anticipated as his artillery prepared for action during the evening of 12 March.

# 7

# BATTLE IS JOINED
## 12–29 MARCH

Below: French paratroopers, probably of 6 BPC, take cover and observe during a patrol.

While it is a truism that work on a military defensive position can never be entirely completed, by Friday 12 March the French troops had by and large achieved all that they could to fortify their still very exposed positions. Only a significant injection of engineer resources could have enabled them to make further significant improvements, and even then the lack of cover or concealment in the valley would have called for a prodigious amount of defence stores if the positions were to be adequately protected from the observed fire that had been falling upon them sporadically since early February. So, as the Viet Minh gunners carried out their final preparations and the French soldiers awoke to another day of patrols, dodging shellfire and digging, the stage was finally set for the next part of the drama that was about to take place at Dien Bien Phu. For the senior French commanders the impending onslaught was not only welcomed as the long-awaited chance to deal the Viet Minh a crushing blow, it was also more or less expected, following a French intelligence report that the Viet Minh had

instructed the local inhabitants to vacate their villages in the valley by midday on Saturday 13 March. Accordingly, and having reckoned that the communists would wish to use the final hours of daylight to adjust their artillery fire, while the onset of darkness would prevent French combat air support, on the evening of Friday 12 March Colonel de Castries concluded his evening briefing conference with the words 'Gentlemen, it's for tomorrow at 1700.' In this assessment both he and French intelligence would be proved absolutely correct.

When Generals Navarre and Cogny took the fateful decision to hold Dien Bien Phu and invite the Viet Minh to attack the base, they surrendered the operational initiative to General Giap, for while the French had chosen the ground, they had conferred upon their enemy the choice of timing. When it became evident in December 1953 that the French were indeed establishing a new position in the Dien Bien Phu valley, Giap's first inclination had been to attack it as soon as practicable. But as more and more French troops and equipment arrived, Giap had realised that a communist victory could not be assured, and a decisive defeat at Dien Bien Phu could set back the wider communist campaign in Indo-China by about five years. Consequently, he had modified his initial operational plan considerably in order to carry out the prolonged build-up of troops and *matériel* that were essential if a communist victory was to be guaranteed.

Giap's attack plan called for a progressive crumbling or imploding of the over-extended French positions. This required the early elimination of what might be termed the outpost positions of Gabrielle, Beatrice and Anne-Marie. The Viet Minh point of main effort was always the cluster of French positions centred on the village of Muong Thanh (Dien Bien Phu), and in light of this a reinforced regiment was deployed to maintain a holding presence about Isabelle to the south until such time as the main French position had been overcome. Giap well understood that he had eventually to close up his infantrymen to the French positions, in order for them to launch direct assaults in overwhelming strength, while at the same time minimising their exposure on open ground to French fire-power and air attack. He also knew that he needed to conclude the battle before the effects of the monsoon rains made his overland supply system even more precarious than the air supply system on which the French garrison depended.

Shells from the ring of guns and mortars that occupied the hillside positions overlooking Dien Bien Phu had been falling regularly since January, and they had inflicted a steady stream of casualties, damaged artillery weapons, destroyed or disabled aircraft and so on throughout the period. But their most important impact was probably the debilitating and morale-sapping effect that this fire had on the French Union soldiers who could neither relax nor move about unobserved above ground. Nevertheless, however irritating this fire may have been, for most members of the garrison it simply presaged the battle which they welcomed as the end of an uncomfortable four months, and the opportunity to inflict a final crushing defeat upon the Viet Minh. At 1700 on Saturday 13 March the French soldiers were disabused of such notions.

The first bombardment fell on Beatrice (or Him Lam as the Viet Minh termed the position). A veritable storm of fire and destruction created by hundreds of shells and mortar bombs crashed on to the inadequately reinforced bunkers, weapon pits and trenches, burying soldiers, weapons and equipment alike. Beatrice was garrisoned by 750 legionnaires of the 3/13 DBLE, commanded by Major Paul Pégot, a combat experienced and élite unit. Despite the martial qualities of its defenders, the weight of artillery fire that fell upon Beatrice was both mind-numbing and physically overwhelming: especially so in light of the lack of engineer resources to improve the position. By 1815 the first lines of assaulting Viet Minh infantry had closed up and were trying to breach the protective minefield. At 1830 the 3/13 DBLE command bunker received a series of direct hits, which killed Major Pégot and all of his battalion headquarters staff.

Despite the shock effect of the bombardment and the elimination of the 3/13 DBLE battalion command team, some legionnaires still managed to inflict casualties on the waves of Viet Minh troops of the 312th Division that were now surging towards them out of the gathering darkness. By about 2030 they had breached the minefields and barbed wire entanglements and had stormed into virtually every part of the devastated position. Satchel charges and grenades neutralised the few remaining pockets of French resistance. Although for all practical purposes Beatrice had fallen by shortly after midnight, it was not until 0200 hours that the last of the surviving legionnaires finally abandoned their shattered position. They concealed themselves in the nearby jungle and worked their way back to the safety of Dominique after first light the next day. Only two junior officers and 192 legionnaires – many of whom were wounded – managed to escape the onslaught and reach the main French positions. The Viet Minh claimed to have taken 200 prisoners, but the number was probably fewer. Although a counterattack by a force of paratroopers of GAP 2, supported by M-24 tanks, was launched to recapture Beatrice at 0730 next morning, it quickly stalled in the face of heavy fire, and there was then a short truce to collect the French casualties on Beatrice. Thereafter, no further attempt was made to regain the lost position: a decision which begged the question of whether or not it had been correct to occupy what had always been a vulnerable position – dominated by the nearby high ground – in the first place.

Although Beatrice bore the brunt of Giap's first attack, artillery shells had fallen all over the French positions, and the ease with which the command posts had been identified and zeroed by the communist artillery observers was exemplified by the destruction of the command post of Lieutenant Colonel Jules Gaucher, who commanded the central sub-sector, which comprised Beatrice and the main Dien Bien Phu position. Soon after 1830 hours a shell landed on the bunker air shaft, penetrated the bunker, exploded and killed or seriously injured almost all the staff therein – including Lieutenant Colonel Gaucher, who sustained horrific injuries and died shortly afterwards. At 1950 hours Colonel de Castries appointed Lieutenant Colonel Pierre Charles Langlais,[19] the energetic commander of GAP 2, as commander of the central sub-sector in place of Gaucher, an appointment that would have a particular influence upon the later conduct of the French Union defence. Langlais was succeeded as commander of GAP 2 by Major Hubert de Séguin-Pazzis.

While the battle for Beatrice was taking place, a heavy weight of artillery fire had also been falling on Gabrielle (Doc Lap), in preparation for an assault on the night of 14 March. Gabrielle was manned by the Algerians of 5/7 RTA, commanded by Major Roland de Mecquenem, who were supported by the mortars of the Foreign Legion's 2 CMMLE.

During the first twenty-four hours of the bombardment the main airstrip had been comprehensively shelled, so that by last light on Sunday 14 March Dien Bien Phu had lost its entire integral air support: fighters, helicopters and observation aircraft alike. But aircraft based at Hanoi and elsewhere were of course still able to support the garrison, albeit after a lengthy flight, and weather permitting. Accordingly, during the afternoon of 14 March, the Vietnamese paratroopers of 5 BPVN, now commanded by Captain André Botella, dropped on to the all too familiar DZs that they had last seen on 22 November when their battalion had taken part in the original Operation 'Castor' parachute drop.[20] These reinforcements were a welcome addition to the garrison, although they did sustain a number of casualties during the drop and their subsequent move to the main position, where they concentrated at strong-point Eliane.

As darkness fell that Sunday evening, two reinforced regiments of Viet Minh from the 308th Division were gradually working their way into the French positions on Gabrielle, many of which were already in ruins as a result of the almost incessant artillery bombardment. But the French artillery laid down a devastating fire on the advancing communist troops and, although they had made some inroads into Gabrielle by about 0230 hours on 15 March, the assault ground to a temporary halt with the Algerian soldiers still in overall possession of the strong-point. One hour later the attack resumed, in the course of which both Major de Mecquenem and Major Kah (who had been due to take over 5/7 RTA just as the communist offensive began) were wounded – Kah severely – when the Viet Minh artillery scored a direct hit on the 5/7 RTA battalion command post. Thus 5/7 RTA lost its battalion command team at about 0430 hours. Meanwhile, the communist infantry continued their attack, and at 0745 hours a final surge overwhelmed the remaining pockets of French resistance. In fact, an *ad hoc* force, comprised of 5 BPVN, a company of 1 BEP and the M-24 tanks, had been put together by Major de Séguin-Pazzis at about 0500 that morning, with a view to reinforcing and if necessary recapturing Gabrielle. But this force came under heavy artillery and infantry fire while moving up, and more than half of 5 BPVN refused to advance. Although the balance of the much reduced force did reach the foot of Gabrielle, it was entirely inadequate to carry out its original task, and so between 0830 and 0900 they withdrew to strong-points Huguette and Anne-Marie, taking with them those few Algerian and Foreign Legion soldiers that had managed to evade death or capture on Gabrielle.

The battle for Gabrielle cost the French Union garrison some 1,000 soldiers dead and missing – including those lost from the ill-fated counter-attack force. 5/7 RTA sustained at least eighty fatalities, with a further 400 soldiers missing. One M-24 tank was badly damaged. But the capability loss was in reality much greater than this, as the newly-arrived 5 BPVN had to all intents and purposes failed its first real test under fire, which (although many of its soldiers subsequently performed their duties well) largely negated its immediate value to the garrison.[21] And this was not all, for Gabrielle had been one of the best constructed of the outlying strong-points – the paucity of engineer stores notwithstanding. The effect upon the rest of the garrison of seeing the defences on Gabrielle destroyed so easily by the Viet Minh artillery, and the position overrun so quickly by their infantrymen, was every bit as significant as the tactical impact of the loss of the strong-point. Although General Giap's 308th Division had suffered losses that exceeded 1,000 dead and up to 3,000 wounded in the battle for Gabrielle, his troops had none the less delivered in short order the tactical victories that were essential to the subsequent success of the operational plan.

At nightfall on Sunday 14 March 1954, Beatrice and Gabrielle no longer existed as part of the Dien Bien Phu position; two battalions – 3/13 DBLE and 5/7 RTA – had been decimated, and a third (5 BPVN) battalion's combat effectiveness called seriously into question. The garrison's on-site combat air support was no more, the main airstrip being under constant and largely uncontested fire of the communist artillery. On the night of 15/16 March[22] the once supremely confident artillery commander at Dien Bien Phu, the one-armed Colonel Charles Piroth – by now a man crushed by the failure of his guns to make any impact upon the communist artillery – went to his bunker, drew the pin from a grenade with his teeth, held the grenade to his chest, released the spring handle, and died. Piroth's somewhat extravagant act of expiation of his professional failure denied Colonel de Castries a deputy commander, and can have done little to boost the confidence of those officers and men constrained to continue the fight. This

Below: The Viet Minh made extensive use of bicycles to move *matériel* over the mountain trails to the communist forces at Dien Bien Phu.

situation was exacerbated by the garrison's chief of staff, Lieutenant Colonel Keller, suffering a nervous breakdown at about the same time; he was later evacuated by an ambulance aircraft on 24 March. Although Colonel de Castries would later attract criticism for his command of Dien Bien Phu, the loss of these two key members of his command team – in neither case as a direct result of enemy action – was undoubtedly a major blow that must have placed an almost intolerable burden upon him right at the start of

Table 17 – FRENCH UNION REINFORCEMENTS PARACHUTED INTO DIEN BIEN PHU BETWEEN 13 AND 29 MARCH 1954

| French Unit Military Designation (main units only) | English Title | Remarks |
|---|---|---|
| 5 BPVN (5e Bataillon de Parachutistes Vietnamiens) | 5th Vietnamese Airborne Battalion | Dropped 14 Mar 54; commanded by Captain (later major) André Botella. |
| 6 BPC (6e Bataillon de Parachutistes Coloniaux) | 6th Colonial Airborne Battalion | Dropped 16 Mar 54; 613 men strong, commanded by Major Marcel 'Bruno' Bigeard. |
| ACP 3 | 3rd Airborne Surgical Team | Commanded by Lieutenant Rézillot. Dropped 14 Mar 54, and was then based at Isabelle. |
| ACP 6 | 6th Airborne Surgical Team | Commanded by Lieutenant Vidal. Dropped 17 Mar 54. |

the main Viet Minh offensive.[23] Colonel Vaillant later succeeded Piroth as commander of the garrison's already reduced artillery and heavy mortar units.

At 1105 hours on Tuesday 16 March, the next major drop of reinforcements was carried out, as the transport aircraft bringing in the first wave of 613 men of 6 BPC arrived above the valley. Reinforcements for 1 BEP, 8 BPC and the artillery units followed, and all the paratroopers were safely within Dien Bien Phu by 1630. While the arrival of these much needed reinforcements, many of whom were élite troops, was of course welcome, of possibly greater significance was the return[24] to Dien Bien Phu of Major Marcel 'Bruno' Bigeard at the head of the 6 BPC. Both Major Bigeard[25] and Lieutenant Colonel Langlais were each destined to play major roles in shaping and conducting much of the rest of the French Union forces' battle in the valley.

The final important success of this first phase of Giap's attack plan for Dien Bien Phu came about almost by default on Wednesday 17 March, with the collapse of most of strong-point Anne-Marie's subordinate positions. This happened when, shortly after first light, most of the T'ai infantrymen of 3 BT simply left their trenches and headed for their homes in the not too distant mountains. Only one 3 BT company plus the legionnaires of the 1 CMMLE stood firm (on Anne-Marie 4), and so strong-point Anne-Marie literally died as a French position, while the emplacements formerly occupied by the T'ai tribesmen were taken over by Viet Minh troops who speedily moved in to fill the vacuum. Thereafter, the defensive perimeter contracted, and Anne-Marie 3 and 4 were absorbed into the Huguette complex of strong-points. No attempt was made to recapture the positions abandoned by 3 BT, and the Viet Minh were thus left in possession of the three hill features within the valley that overlooked the airstrip, the main command post and the principal complex of French positions at Dien Bien Phu to their north-west, north and east.

Quite apart from the fact that their occupation of what they termed Ban Keo now enabled the Viet Minh to bring accurate artillery fire to bear on the main airstrip (the runway was forced to close, although a last evacuation of casualties by air was achieved by a single transport aircraft on 27 March), the demise of 3 BT and Anne-Marie was particularly significant for two even more profound reasons. First and foremost, it was an unequivocal victory for the communist propaganda campaign that Giap had long directed against the non-French troops at Dien Bien Phu – the Indo-Chinese and North Africans in particular. The effort allocated to this psychological operation was reinforced and it continued to degrade the resolve and loyalty of the remaining T'ai units in the garrison. Next, the desertion of the T'ai soldiers highlighted the organisational weakness of a garrison in which more than 50 per cent of the soldiers were neither metropolitan French nor Foreign Legion; with a majority of these non-French troops having close local and family ties to the area in which they were now required to fight. Although many of these men had – and would again – fight bravely for France, their particular circumstances and origins left them wide open to communist propaganda that emphasised and questioned the apparent injustice of non-Frenchmen being required to fight and die in order to maintain a French colonial empire that subjugated them to the whims and aspirations of a distant government in Paris. This potent argument had been strengthened immeasurably by the National Assembly's decision, made in the wake of the disaster at Cao Bang in September and October 1950, that conscripted French soldiers would not be sent to serve in Indo-China or indeed on active service elsewhere overseas: which meant that the war in Indo-China would inevitably be fought in the main by locally recruited troops and by units recruited from France's North African territories, and by the Foreign Legion. The extent of the complacency of the Paris government and military high command in Paris over the needs, feelings and motivation of the thousands of non-French troops under their command was remarkable, and provided General Giap and the Viet Minh with an extremely powerful propaganda weapon: one that was exploited to the full. The operational success of this weapon could be specifically quantified on 17 March 1954, when it effected the removal of almost an entire infantry battalion from the French Union forces' order of battle at Dien Bien Phu without the need of an assault. On the same day, two legionnaires of the 3/13 DBLE, that had been decimated on 13 March, deserted to the enemy, an indicator of the shock and growing sense of unease now manifest in some parts of the garrison.

With Beatrice, Gabrielle and most of Anne-Marie firmly in Viet Minh hands, General Giap had, in just four days, changed irrevocably the physical shape of the French defensive positions. He had almost entirely negated the original French battle plan, and ensured that its subsequent course would continue – at the operational level – to be determined by the Viet Minh. As the major communist assaults of those first few days came to an end, the fighting settled into a form of fluid siege warfare, as both sides took stock of the changed situation and sought to maintain or regain the tactical initiative. But, short of intervention from outside, tactical initiatives were all that Colonel de Castries (and, after 16 March,

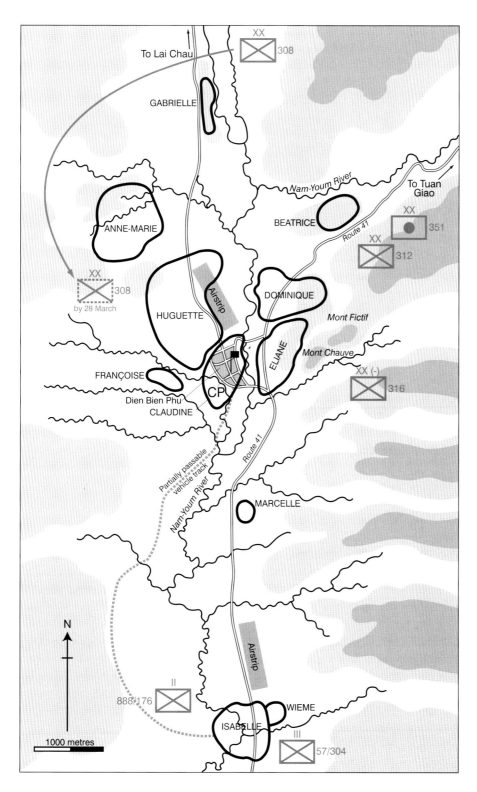

**DIEN BIEN PHU VALLEY: SITUATION 13 MARCH 1954**

To Lai Chau

XX 308

GABRIELLE

Nam-Youm River

To Tuan Giao

ANNE-MARIE

BEATRICE

Route 41

XX 351

XX 312

XX 308
by 28 March

Airstrip

DOMINIQUE

Mont Fictif

HUGUETTE

ELIANE

Mont Chauve

FRANÇOISE

CP

XX (-) 316

Dien Bien Phu
CLAUDINE

Partially passable
vehicle track

Nam-Youm River

Route 41

MARCELLE

N

1000 metres

II
888/176

Airstrip

WIEME

ISABELLE

III
57/304

increasingly the two airborne commanders Lieutenant Colonel Langlais and Major Bigeard) could aspire to, as the French Union forces within the valley could never regain the operational or strategic initiative without such intervention or support.

While the French Union force losses had been considerable, the Viet Minh had also suffered very heavy losses during the opening days of the battle, and after the fall of Anne-Marie no more major ground assaults were launched by the communists for almost two weeks. But although there was a temporary pause in the infantry attacks, the artillery fire continued incessantly. Three days after the main airstrip closed, the main transit road within Dien Bien Phu also became unusable. Meanwhile, the French air force remained generally unable to locate and strike the communist artillery positions. At the same time the artillery within the garrison still could not engage these guns which were progressively destroying its infrastructure, denying it re-supply and grinding the very ground it occupied into an undulating desert of talcum-fine sand. The battle was now assuming many of the characteristics of the sieges of an earlier age; with the Viet Minh's bombardments, propaganda campaign, infiltrations and entrenching work relieved only by occasional, but usually intense and violent, direct clashes of arms.

Simultaneous with the battle for Dien Bien Phu, both sides were engaged in the vital logistics struggle: the French, from the air; the Viet Minh, on the trails that led southwards from the Chinese border. In parallel with this the French were under constant and growing pressure to evacuate their growing numbers of wounded. Evacuations were achieved whenever possible, but only through the sheer courage and skill of the small number of French pilots who braved the perils of attempted landing on the Dien Bien Phu airstrip, or elsewhere on the position by helicopter.

The summary at table 18 highlights some of the more significant events of the closing weeks of March 1954, a period which saw daily exchanges of artillery and mortar fire, patrol actions and many instances of close combat.

On 29 March the first monsoon rains fell and continued unabated, accompanied by persistent banks of low dense cloud that further disrupted the already problematical supply drops. Much of the *matériel* (probably about 30 per cent in total) that was dispatched to Dien Bien Phu by parachute fell well outside the defensive perimeter, directly into the hands of the Viet Minh. Meanwhile, water flooded into the underground passages, bunkers and trenches, making the daily existence of the French Union soldiers one of continuous danger from the shell-fire above ground and of unrelieved misery underground, because of the sea of red mud in which they were now constrained to live, fight and – in many cases – to die.

General Giap's troops were also experiencing similar if not quite such extreme privations in their emplacements about Dien Bien Phu. Not withstanding their ideological commitment, the Viet Minh soldiers' attitudes had been

**Table 18 – SIGNIFICANT EVENTS, 18 – 29 MARCH 1954**

| Date | Summary of Event or Action | Remarks |
|------|---------------------------|---------|
| 18 Mar | Viet Minh positions dug south of Eliane extended to the Nam-Youm River and so cut the main vehicle road to Isabelle. | Isabelle, commanded by Lieutenant Colonel André Lalande, effectively isolated from routine support from the main French position. |
| 19 Mar | Decision taken by de Castries (for security reasons) to expel the remaining T'ai civilians from the valley villages with effect 20 Mar. | Nevertheless, the civilian family members of a number of Meo tribesmen of GC 8 and GMPT 1 remained within the positions. There were also within the garrison the civilians of two Bordels Mobiles de Campagne (BMC) – mobile field brothels – one of which was staffed by Vietnamese girls, the other by Algerian girls of the Ouled Naïl tribe. These girls remained throughout the battle, many later serving as nurses in the field hospital, in often appalling conditions. |
| 21 Mar | 6 BPC reconnaissance sortie along Route 41. | Confirmed extent and cohesion of Viet Minh build-up. |
| 20–22 Mar | A 1 BEP battlegroup (led by Captain François Vieulles), including M-24 tanks, eventually re-opened the road to Isabelle, but with 151 dead, 72 wounded and one man missing. | Viet Minh casualties (of the 304th Division's Infantry Regiment No. 57) were very heavy, but despite this and the 1 BEP battlegroup's success, unconstrained road access to Isabelle could no longer be guaranteed. |
| 23 Mar | Major napalm attack (Operation 'Neptune') carried out by French air force against Viet Minh trenches about Dien Bien Phu and (Operation 'Eole') Route 41. | Despite their impressive scale no significant destruction to the communist forces was discerned. |
| 24 Mar | Lieutenant Colonel Langlais and his airborne commanders and staffs assumed de facto tactical command of the entire Dien Bien Phu position, while de Castries maintained operational and presentational command, and responsibility for direct liaison with the high command in Hanoi. The new, simplified, tactical command structure of Dien Bien Phu was: ● Commander: Lieutenant Colonel Langlais (overall command and of Sector East) ● Deputy: Lieutenant Colonel Lemeunier ● Sector West: Lieutenant Colonel Voinot ● GAP 2: Major Séguin-Pazzis ● Counter-attack force: Major Bigeard (Captain Thomas assumed command of 6 BPC) ● Tactical reserve: Captain Philippe ● Isabelle: Colonel Lalande | The whole shape and nature of the French defence had changed significantly since 12 Mar and the need to manage and if possible reverse a worsening situation was undoubtedly better suited to the professional talents and style of Lieutenant Colonel Langlais, Major Bigeard and the paratroopers of GAP 2 rather than to the understandably more conventional de Castries and the now almost unrecognisable garrison organisation of the original defence plan. This remarkable change of the French command arrangements was generally achieved amicably within Dien Bien Phu, where all concerned perhaps already understood that an extraordinary and declining military situation justified such extraordinary measures. Notwithstanding this, some difficulties stemmed from Langlais' concept of constant offensive action, while de Castries continued to advocate primarily defensive action to buy time for the garrison to be saved by external intervention. This divergence of perception in many ways mirrored at the tactical level the separate views of Dien Bien Phu expressed by Navarre and Cogny at the operational level during the closing months of the previous year. |
| 24 Mar | 1/ 2 REI and 6 BPC sorties. | Further confirmed extent of Viet Minh build-up. Road to Isabelle cut again. |
| 25 Mar | 1/4 RTM re-open road to Isabelle. | Aided by the 3/1 RCC M-24 tank platoon from Isabelle. |
| 27 Mar | A C-47, piloted by Captain Bourgereau, took off from Dien Bien Phu with 19 wounded aboard. | This was the last such flight to depart Dien Bien Phu successfully. Several other C-47s had already been shot down en route in or out or destroyed on the airstrip. Subsequently some further flights did land, but none took off; their surviving crew members joined the garrison. One such crew member was French air force nurse Lieutenant Geneviève de Galard-Terraube, who then served with distinction at the main hospital until the end of the battle and was later accorded the title 'Angel of Dien Bien Phu' by the media of the time. |
| 28 Mar | A major sortie by 6 BPC, 8 BPC, 1 BEP, supported by all artillery and M-24s, plus air force fighters, was instigated by de Castries and planned and led by Bigeard to destroy Viet Minh anti-aircraft positions west of Dien Bien Phu, carried out 0600–1500. | Despite French casualties of 20 dead and 90 wounded, the attack was a complete success, and vindicated to a great extent Langlais' wider concept of an 'offensive defence'. The Viet Minh (mainly soldiers from Infantry Regiment No. 36, of the 308th Division) lost 350 dead, 10 captured, plus five anti-aircraft guns, twelve .50 HMGs, two anti-tank rocket launchers and a large quantity of small-arms. But the French were too few to be able to occupy and hold the hard-won ground. |
| 29 Mar | Re-structuring of positions at Dominique and Claudine to create strong-points Épervier (8 BPC plus quad-.50 HMGs, commanded by Major Tourret) and Junon (elements of 1 BEP and others, commanded by Major Guiraud). | Intention to strengthen defences on the hill features to the east of the main position. All the Eliane positions were strengthened and reinforced at the same time. Meanwhile, to the south, Isabelle was finally cut off from the main position by the Viet Minh. |

influenced and modified by their experiences during the previous four months of fighting. For some, there was a growing awareness of the sheer scale of the casualties sustained by the communist divisions thus far, allied to a general fatigue that had begun to sap the morale of some individuals and units alike. For others, the slow but sure successes (especially those of mid-March) enjoyed by the PAVN troops had bred an excess of confidence similar to that which had bedevilled the French high command at the close of 1953, and which was now potentially just as injurious to the combat effectiveness of the Viet Minh divisions at Dien Bien Phu as it had already proved to be for the French. But as March drew to a close, after the two weeks' respite enjoyed by the majority of his forces, the time had come for Giap to launch his next major offensive. Having already isolated Isabelle and secured the west, north and north-western approaches to (and exits from) the Dien Bien Phu valley, General Giap now turned his attention to the five hill features that lay immediately to the east of the main French position, which were the keys both to its security and to French access to the airstrip. The importance that Giap attached to this next phase of the campaign is underlined by his decision to assume direct command of the impending battle in the valley from his chief of staff, General Hoang Van Thai, who had implemented Giap's direction and orders for the conduct of the tactical battle thus far. At this stage the Chinese Generals Li Cheng-hu and Wei Guo-qing were Giap's principal advisers: further evidence of the escalating aid for, and influence upon, the Viet Minh from the People's Republic of China.

Coincidentally, Colonel de Castries and Lieutenant Colonel Langlais had decided that Langlais would be flown out of Dien Bien Phu on one of the casualty evacuation aircraft scheduled to arrive on the night of 29 March, so that he could brief Major General Cogny in Hanoi personally about the deteriorating situation, and secure the high command's unequivocal commitment to hold Dien Bien Phu in any and all circumstances, with the provision of the unlimited support that this implied. This accomplished, Langlais planned to return next day and drop into Dien Bien Phu by parachute – a risky business at the best of times. However, no more aircraft were able to land at the base and so Langlais was unable to leave that night: an eventuality that – at the tactical level – was undoubtedly fortuitous in light of the renewed onslaught that General Giap had planned for the following day. Indeed, it is questionable whether or not the Langlais mission would have produced the desired result in any case and, in hindsight, it is remarkable that de Castries was prepared to countenance one of his two most effective commanders leaving a Dien Bien Phu garrison that was already in crisis. Either he recognised the true extent of that crisis and judged the risk worthwhile, or else he still did not fully realise the dire situation in which the garrison now found itself. On the other hand, he may simply have been holding firm to his original belief that the garrison would, eventually – and *in extremis* – be saved by external intervention, French or international.

# CLOSE COMBAT
## 30 MARCH – 5 APRIL

Although it would certainly be incorrect to characterise the wider battle of Dien Bien Phu as one that was fought by a single category of French Union unit or ethnic group – such as the Foreign Legion, the airborne or parachute troops ('Les Paras'), the German legionnaires, or the Algerians, Moroccans, or Vietnamese – one particular phase of the ensuing battle did with some justification become identified with one such group. This was the intense and violent period of combat that began when Giap resumed his offensive on the afternoon of Tuesday 30 March, and which had generally concluded on Eliane by the night of 1 April, although the fighting continued elsewhere virtually unabated for four days and nights. This time the main Viet Minh assault fell directly upon the eastern strong-points of Dominique and Eliane, both of which were manned primarily by soldiers of the airborne battalions. It was launched from the cover afforded by the two hills that had been dubbed by the French 'Mont Fictif' ('Phoney Hill') and 'Mont Chauve' ('Bald Hill'). These were separated from the main positions on Eliane by the open ground known as the 'Champs-Élysées', across which the French had dug and manned some lines of trenches.

At 1700 hours the communist artillery rained shells on to the main headquarters, Eliane and Dominique. The fire missions developed into a rolling barrage, behind which the bulk of the infantrymen of the 312th and 316th Divisions rose from their earthworks and surged towards the French emplacements. Initially, the assault was irresistible.

On Dominique, the T'ai and Algerian units quickly collapsed in the face of the human tide that breached the minefields and wire in short order and then fell

Below: From the outset, the fate of Dien Bien Phu depended upon its combat air support. Here a Bearcat fighter (with two others visible in the background) takes off from the airstrip during the days before the Viet Minh artillery destroyed these aircraft and rendered the airstrip unusable.

upon them, grenading their bunkers and fighting along their trenches. To arrest the growing débâcle, a company commander of 5 BPVN, aptly named Lieutenant Martinet, ordered his paratroopers to shoot any Algerian or T'ai soldiers who left their post. These paratroopers, together with many of the Algerian battalion's junior commanders and the remaining Foreign Legion mortar company crewmen, stood and fought to the last man. By 2150 hours 3/3 RTA no longer existed and positions Dominique 1 and 2 were in the hands of the Viet Minh soldiers of the 312th Division. But as the waves of communist troops rolled on towards Dominique 3 and the gun positions there, the Algerian artillerymen of 4/2/4 RAC depressed the barrels of their 105mm howitzers and fired shell after shell directly into the massed infantry at ranges of less than 1,000 metres. Simultaneously, the two multi-barrelled quad-.50cal HMGs emplaced on Épervier engaged the right flank of the advancing Viet Minh infantry, checking them and pushing them into an adjacent minefield. The combined efforts of the French artillery battery and the HMGs halted the attack and left more than 200 Viet Minh dead on the battlefield. During the remaining hours of darkness the survivors sought cover in the immediate area as best they could.

Meanwhile, Giap's 316th Division, reinforced by two regiments of the 308th Division (including the élite Infantry Regiment No. 102, the 'Capital' regiment), was contesting possession of the positions on Eliane. As the shells rained down, and an awareness of the collapse of 3/3 RTA on Dominique spread, some of the Moroccan soldiers of 1/4 RTM on Eliane 1 began to desert their posts, but on Eliane 4 the Vietnamese paratroopers of 5 BPVN were holding, as was the bulk of 1/4 RTM on Eliane 2. As the night drew on, the French positions at Champs-Élysées and much of Eliane 2 had already ceased to exist, having finally succumbed to the powerful artillery bombardment and massed infantry assaults. The French situation was precarious, and at about 2300 Langlais lost radio contact with 1/4 RTM, implying the loss of Eliane 2 to the Viet Minh.

Although the situation was dire, all was certainly not yet lost. In fact, 1/4 RTM was still holding, but Langlais' radio had simply wandered off frequency. Luckily Major Bigeard – ever mindful of his counter-attack role – had been monitoring the 1/4 RTM radio net and realised that the battalion was still holding. He informed Langlais accordingly, and also sent a company of paratroopers to reinforce the Moroccan battalion. Bigeard's message was timely, because shortly after midnight, two young airborne officers, Lieutenant Lucciani and Lieutenant Fournier, led an *ad hoc* counter-attack force comprised of legionnaires, paratroopers, Moroccans and others, together with a couple of M-24 tanks, to recapture the ground from Eliane 4 to Eliane 2. Had Bigeard not confirmed the continued presence of 1/4 RTM on Eliane 2, Langlais was about to order the full weight of French artillery fire on to that hill, which would not only have decimated the surviving Moroccan soldiers, but also prejudiced the French counter-attack. The latter involved several hours of close combat and exceptional violence, but left the French soldiers in control of the ground, with several hundred more dead communist troops littering the surrounding area. While the desperate fight for Eliane continued, an equally bitter struggle for the Huguette positions to the north and west of the airstrip had also ensued, but here too, despite the vastly superior numbers of Viet Minh, these positions were still in French hands as dawn broke on Wednesday, 31 March.

With the Viet Minh clearly still capable of continuing the offensive, the French commanders had already planned to launch a coordinated counter-attack by GAP 2, plus 3/3 REI from Isabelle. The counter-attack force was to be drawn from 5 BPVN, 6 BPC and 8 BPC. The 3/1 RCC tanks from both the main position and from Isabelle would support the attack, together with all available artillery, and the aim of this operation was to restore overall French control of those tactically vital sectors of Dominique and Eliane which were still occupied by the communists. Implicit in the plan was an assumption that further paratroop units would reinforce Dien Bien Phu once the weather permitted this. And as that Wednesday drew on, the torrential rain that had fallen incessantly since 29 March eased and eventually stopped.

The force from 3/3 REI had set out from Isabelle at dawn, but eventually encountered a major part of Infantry Regiment No. 57 (of the 304th Division) a couple of kilometres north of the strong-point. The Viet Minh blocking position proved impenetrable, and with fifteen dead and missing, plus fifty wounded, the legionnaires, covered by the tanks, had been forced to conduct a fighting withdrawal back to Isabelle by early afternoon. This effectively wrote them out of the original counter-attack plan and confirmed yet again the true extent of Isabelle's operational isolation. Meanwhile, despite the welcome break in the weather, there was still no sign of the much-awaited troop transports in the skies above Dien Bien Phu, as the GAP 2 units moved off at 1330 hours.

Soon after 1430 hours, 8 BPC re-occupied the devastated Dominique 2. Then, half an hour later, 5 BPVN and 6 BPC reported that they had successfully recaptured Eliane 1. But both positions now began to sustain rising numbers of casualties from heavy artillery fire, as the Viet Minh prepared their own bid to recapture the hills. There was still no sign of the desperately-needed reinforcements, although it was generally known that three airborne battalions were ready to deploy from the airhead at Hanoi. In yet another indictment of its feeble support of Dien Bien Phu, the high command[26] in Hanoi failed to react opportunely to the garrison's need of reinforcements, and so must bear a considerable amount of indirect responsibility for that which followed.

With no reinforcement in prospect, and having been authorised to do so, at 1530 hours 8 BPC reluctantly withdrew from the hard-won Dominique 2. This precipitated a domino effect which resulted in Eliane 1 having to be abandoned by the 5 BPVN and 6 BPC soldiers, and the Viet Minh rushed forward to re-occupy these positions virtually unopposed. The three remaining 105mm guns of the artillery battery that had done such sterling work the previous night were also forced to withdraw into the main position, as the territory held by the French union troops – and consequently the area into which reinforcements and *matériel* could be dropped – contracted once again. The successful counter-attack of 31 March had undoubtedly inflicted significant casualties on the Viet Minh, but French losses had also been heavy, and the communists were far better able to absorb them. Meanwhile, the French Union paratroops had been forced to relinquish all the ground that they had recaptured that afternoon.

The Viet Minh attack on Eliane – now held by a composite group of individuals and sub-units from 1/4 RTM, 1/2 REI and 1 BEP – resumed at nightfall. Wave after wave of green-clad infantrymen, dressed in assault order and topped off by their familiar woven bamboo and fibre helmets, debouched from Mont Chauve, and surged towards the French positions. En route they had to traverse the earlier killing ground of Champs-Élysées, still littered with hundreds of communist bodies. Only the timely intervention of the tanks of the 3/1 RCC at about midnight prevented the massed Viet Minh troops from swamping the French defenders. Remarkably, at dawn on Thursday, 1 April, 6 BPC were still holding Eliane 4, part of Eliane 2 remained under French control, and 8 BPC were still holding Dominique 3. By the end of that morning, since the evening of 30 March, the battle had cost 6 BPC forty-six dead and 183 wounded, and 1 BEP had lost forty dead, 189 wounded and eight missing. The battle of 'Les Paras' for the Eliane positions from 30 March to 1 April had cost these two battalions, together with 8 BPC and 5 BPVN, dearly; and there was still no sign of the expected reinforcements.

### The Fight for the Western Hills

Below: A column of French Union troops moving to new positions alongside the main airstrip. Note the dominating high ground in the background.

On the west side of the base, despite the huge numbers of Viet Minh assault troops hurled against it, Huguette was still in French hands on 1 April, thanks largely to a valiant and spirited defence by a single company from 5 BPVN. But to the south-west, strong-point Françoise simply ceased to exist when the T'ai soldiers based there finally decided that they had had enough and began to desert their positions. Fortunately this was a relatively gradual process over the afternoon of 1 April, which permitted legionnaires of 1/2 REI to recover the T'ai's

support weapons. Langlais dealt with these T'ai deserters much as he had with the errant Vietnamese soldiers of 5 BPVN on 15 March. He disarmed them and relegated them to work as coolies, although many simply disappeared and joined a rapidly growing and incongruous group of several hundred North African and Vietnamese deserters, together with a few Frenchmen and some legionnaires, who by now were inhabiting a veritable warren of caves and tunnels on the banks of the Nam-Youm River within the main position. As their numbers increased, these 'internal deserters' were derided as the 'Rats of the Nam-Youm' by the other French Union soldiers.[27]

In Hanoi, the decision had at last been taken to order the dropping of reinforcements. Although Langlais and Bigeard urgently needed airborne battalions dropped as complete units, the military and air force staff in Hanoi advised Major General Cogny that these drops should only be carried out piecemeal, by night, in the interests of the aircraft and the precious loads they carried. They also resisted the Dien Bien Phu commanders' pragmatic request for drops to be deposited directly on to the main defensive position, rather than on formal DZs; the headquarters staff's doctrinaire stance was becoming less tenable with each passing day. In any event, between the nights of Thursday 1 April and Wednesday 14 April, these reinforcements did finally arrive at Dien Bien Phu. Most of the drops arrived during the virtually continuous fighting about the Huguette positions, and inevitably some sticks of paratroopers and *matériel* landed in Viet Minh-controlled areas. The following units dropped into Dien Bien Phu during this fortnight:

**Table 19 – FRENCH UNION REINFORCEMENTS PARACHUTED INTO DIEN BIEN PHU BETWEEN 1 AND 14 APRIL 1954**

| French Unit Military Designation (main units only) | English Title | Remarks |
|---|---|---|
| 2/1 RCP (2e Bataillon, 1er Régiment de Chasseurs Parachutistes) | 2nd Battalion, 1st Airborne Light Infantry Regiment | Dropped between 1 and 5 Apr 54. Commanded by Major Jean Bréchignac. |
| 35 RALP (35e Régiment d'Artillerie Légère Parachutiste) | 35th Airborne Light Artillery Regiment | Elements only. Dropped between 1 and 11 Apr 54. |
| 2 BEP (2e Bataillon Étranger de Parachutistes) | 2nd Foreign Legion Airborne Battalion | Dropped between 9 and 11 Apr 54. Commanded by Major Hubert Liesenfelt. |
| ACP 5 | 5th Airborne Surgical Team | Commanded by Captain Hantz. Arrived night 13/14 Apr 54. |

Strong attacks were launched against the northern Huguette positions by the PAVN 312th Division at 2200 hours on 1 April, in a bid to gain total control of the airstrip. Although the French positions were overrun, a counter-attack by troops of 1/2 REI and 5 BPVN, supported by three M-24s, restored French control to Huguette 7. But the inadequate rate of reinforcement build-up as of that night meant that this position had once again to be abandoned at 0805 hours on 2 April by those who had just recaptured it. Meanwhile, to the east of Dien Bien Phu,

Major Guiraud had been wounded during a counter-attack by 1 BEP at Champs-Élysées. He was replaced as battalion commander by Captain François Vieulles. Throughout Dien Bien Phu, tactical commanders were progressively being replaced by their subordinates as more and more leaders were wounded.

At 0500 on Saturday 3 April the communists comprehensively destroyed the wire entanglements around Huguette 1 with explosives, and the 100 legionnaires in their trenches and bunkers on the now isolated Huguette 6 – one of the keys to control of the airstrip – realised that the Viet Minh were preparing to strike them next. Part of this preparation was psychological: the deliberate repatriation by the communists of the dead bodies of four horrifically mutilated French soldiers so shocked some of these legionnaires that twelve of them abandoned their weapons and deserted that same afternoon, determined that they would not remain to suffer a similar fate once the position fell to the Viet Minh. Sure enough, the attack came at 1925, but a counter-attack supported by three M-24s launched from Épervier into the flank of the Viet Minh 312th Division caused great slaughter and forced the communists to withdraw. At dawn on 4 April Huguette 6 was still held by the French, and the value of the all too small numbers of tanks available to de Castries, Langlais and Bigeard had been proved yet again. Even the monsoon rains that had fallen without pause until 31 March had continued to fall intermittently rather than constantly, and on the morning of 4 April the heavy, dampening cloud base had also lifted. As the newly arrived 2/1 RCP troopers moved to occupy positions on Dominique and Eliane the Viet Minh withdrew from Eliane 2. An unnatural lull fell over the battlefield, the watery sunshine providing some welcome warmth, but at the same time unwelcome for its effect upon the almost 2,000 Viet Minh and 300 French bodies that still lay on the hillsides of Eliane and across the length and breadth of Champs-Élysées. Apart from a continuing fire-fight at Isabelle (during which that position's eleven 105mm howitzers had suffered particularly heavily from communist artillery fire – with nine guns still operational, but with only six gun crews left), Sunday 4 April proved to be a period of relative respite for both sides, as they took stock of the full extent of the losses they had suffered during the previous three days. But these hours proved to be no more than the lull before the storm.

### The Battle for Huguette 6

With darkness came both a renewal of the monsoon rains, re-doubled in their intensity, and a resumption of the attack on Huguette, the latter marking the end of the concerted offensive that had begun with the battle of 'Les Paras' on Eliane. By 2200 the Huguette positions were under heavy bombardment, with reports of Viet Minh infantry massing for an assault on the already battered Huguette 6 and its garrison of ninety legionnaires, commanded by Lieutenants Rastouil and François. The communist onslaught began soon after 2200, and by 0030 on 5 April the gallant band of defenders, which had by now been reinforced by a 1/13 DBLE company, was under attack from every point of the compass except the south, and had been forced back into the southernmost trenches and bunkers of Huguette 6. They were facing the four battalions of a full PAVN regiment (Infantry Regiment No. 165 of the 312th Division), which was supported by the 120mm mortars of the 308th Division's heavy weapons company and most of the communist artillery that was able to engage the position.

Remarkably, the dwindling band of legionnaires held on. Efforts to reinforce and assist them were made at 0115 by a company of 8 BPC supported by two M-24s.[28] These reached Huguette 6, but could not move further forward against the weight of Viet Minh that opposed them. Clearly more help was required. At 0315 elements of the newly arrived company of 2/1 RCP, commanded by Captain Clédic, worked its way towards the fight and launched an inspired counter-attack straight across the airfield from Épervier, which smashed into the Viet Minh flank at 0420. This spirited action broke the Viet Minh unit upon which it fell, allowed the 2/1 RCP paratroopers to link up with the remaining twenty or so survivors of the Huguette 6 garrison, and enabled the new arrivals to begin clearing the communists from the other trenches and bunkers. It was a defining moment in this phase of the battle.

Although Huguette 6 was once more firmly in French hands, it was still under attack by more than 3,000 Viet Minh soldiers, and the time had come for a full counter-attack against them. Predictably, Bigeard met the requirement.

At 0600, just an hour after Langlais had briefed him on his mission, Bigeard launched a coordinated attack which involved two companies of 6 BPC, with 1 BEP in reserve. Battle was joined just as the communists threw a fourth battalion into the attack, but the cover of darkness had gone, and the paratroopers, legionnaires and French artillery were able to inflict great destruction upon the massed Viet Minh troops now exposed to view on the open ground. At 0830, just as the masses of communist soldiers had begun to waver, French ground-attack aircraft roared into the valley and strafed and bombed the multiple targets presented to them. By 1015 on Monday 5 April, Huguette 6 was again indisputably under French control; although just two weeks later it would again be the focus of intense fighting, and was destined eventually to be abandoned at no little cost. However, on that Monday morning, almost 1,000 dead Viet Minh soldiers lay within and about the position, and many more had undoubtedly been wounded. Twenty-one Viet Minh prisoners had been taken, and PAVN Colonel Thuy's Infantry Regiment No. 165 had – albeit temporarily – been rendered operationally non-effective.

The French Union troops engaged had lost some 200 men in the fight for Huguette 6, including the majority of those legionnaires who had throughout held the position against the odds. But the implications of these losses were much greater for the French, who were forced to rely on a mere trickle of air-dropped reinforcements, while General Giap could – and did – call on reinforcements that were able to move up relatively unimpeded from concentration areas that contained in total some 25,000 reserves. Indeed, by 5 April 1954 the PAVN divisions engaged at Dien Bien Phu had already lost more than 10,000 men since the beginning of the year.

While the eventual outcome of the battle of Dien Bien Phu was all but inevitable, a communist victory was already proving very costly, and its price would rise considerably before it was finally achieved. Having failed to overrun the Eliane and Huguette positions by the massed infantry attacks so favoured by some of his Chinese advisers, General Vo Nguyen Giap now chose to revert to the time-consuming but infinitely safer and more certain siege tactics of old. The Viet Minh began to advance their trenches ever closer to the French fortifications around both the main position and the beleaguered garrison – now numbering just 1,613 men – at Isabelle. Meanwhile the reinforcement of Giap's depleted divisions with new manpower and *matériel* was proceeding apace, and additional communist units, artillery and equipment were arriving to occupy the hills and valleys about Dien Bien Phu. All these still had to run the gauntlet of French air attacks as they made their way to the sound of the guns in that embattled valley, and many newly recruited Viet Minh soldiers were killed before they had an opportunity to fight the French. Indeed, had French combat air-power been directed almost entirely at the Viet Minh lines of communication, rather than against the communist artillery and other positions about the valley, French air force losses of fighters and bombers might have been fewer, and the success of General Giap's logistic plan would undoubtedly have been severely degraded.

Below: The Viet Minh air defences in the hills above Dien Bien Phu were a key contributor to the communist victory.

# SHAPING THE FINAL BATTLE

Although it featured several instances of violent combat, the remaining three weeks of April were characterised by the Viet Minh build-up in preparation for what Giap was determined would be the final assault, and by the French garrison's attempts to halt and reverse the progress of the communist siege trenches that were moving inexorably towards their defence works, while all the time hoping that massive reinforcement or international (by which they meant American) military intervention would yet save the day. Throughout the period 6 to 30 April, Langlais and Bigeard continued to inspire the Dien Bien Phu garrison and to direct its actions.

Table 20 – SIGNIFICANT EVENTS, 6 – 23 APRIL 1954

| Date | Summary of Event or Action | Remarks |
|---|---|---|
| 6 Apr | The final (unplanned) landing of an aircraft at Dien Bien Phu occurred, when a Morane-500 Cricket observation aircraft of 23 GAOA was hit by AA fire and made an emergency landing. | The observer (Lieutenant Choue de La Mestrie) died, the pilot (Sergent-Pilot Ribière) was wounded but rescued, and the aircraft was destroyed on the airstrip. |
| 7 Apr | Successful attack by troops at Isabelle to clear trenches approaching the strong-point. | The main position, apart from the artillery, could no longer assist or affect events at Isabelle. |
| | Mass desertion attempted by remaining T'ai soldiers of 3 BT from Huguette 2. | Those T'ai who had not disappeared were disarmed by paratroopers of 5 BPVN and sent to join the 'Rats of the Nam-Youm'. Those T'ai still willing to fight were sent to join the artillery crews. |
| 9 Apr | Successful air drop of 180 tons of *matériel*, with only 18 tons lost; also first part of 2 BEP arrived. | These events enabled Bigeard to plan a viable counter-attack to recapture Eliane 1. |
| 8–14 Apr | Construction of new complex of positions (Lily) by 1/4 RTM to the SW of Claudine and Huguette, part of which it absorbed. | This construction of new positions, together with continuing offensive action by the French, were clear indicators of the high morale and positive view that persisted in most units; notwithstanding the T'ai desertions of 7 Apr. |
| 10–11 Apr | Major counter-attack launched at 0550 by Bigeard, using 6 BPC, four M-24s, all available artillery, plus combat air support, to retake Eliane 1: which was recaptured at 1400, at a cost of 13 killed, 26 wounded and 10 missing (of an assault force that had numbered originally no more than 170 men). | Two companies of 2/1 RCP relieved the 6 BPC paratroopers at 1600, and bore the brunt of a counter-attack by the three battalions of a full regiment (Infantry Regiment No. 98, 316th Division) at 1845, later reinforced by a fourth battalion. During a night of desperate fighting on Eliane 1, soldiers of 2/1 RCP, 1 BEP and 5 BPVN held, then threw back the Viet Minh. By dawn, communist losses exceeded 400; French losses of dead, wounded and missing numbered almost 200. |
| 11–12 Apr | Viet Minh attack on Eliane 1 by two battalions (Nos. 215 and 439) of PAVN Infantry Regiment No. 98 at last light. Attack defeated by 0700, but French casualties totalled 132. | |
| 11–18 Apr | Increasing numbers of reports of low morale in the Viet Minh forces, including disobedience, and refusals to advance until threatened by being fired on by their own artillery. | The effectiveness of French air force interdiction of Viet Minh lines of communication, the huge casualties already sustained at the hands of the French garrison, the considerable hardships suffered by living semi-underground for months, together with minimal medical aid (one surgeon and six general practitioners for about 50,000 men!), together brought a number of communist units close to mutiny. This, and the debilitating effects of the monsoon on his reinforcement and re-supply arrangements, ensured that Giap reverted to siege tactics in April. |
| 12 Apr | At 1200 a French air force B-26 bomber attacked Épervier by mistake. | Initially, fears were expressed by Langlais that the PRC air force had entered the battle in support of the Viet Minh. Several air attacks were carried out in error against Dien Bien Phu by French aircraft, in addition to the many mis-dropped loads from the cargo aircraft during the battle. The problem increased throughout April, as the Viet Minh flak grew more intense and the perimeter of Dien Bien Phu contracted. |

**Table 20 – SIGNIFICANT EVENTS, 6 – 23 APRIL 1954** (continued)

| Date | Summary of Event or Action | Remarks |
|---|---|---|
| 14 Apr | Viet Minh trenches dug across most of the airstrip, which enabled the communist anti-aircraft guns to move much closer to the garrison's internal DZ.<br><br>That evening, Viet Minh artillery destroyed the garrison's main food dump, forcing it on to short rations from 15 Apr and half rations from 29 Apr.<br><br>Despite the nominal overall strength of the garrison, de Castries (or Langlais) reported to Hanoi that about 3,500 combat-capable soldiers now held the main position. | In addition to communist progress on the ground, French intelligence units reported the following reinforcements either ordered to Dien Bien Phu or requested from the PRC:<br><br>– Elements of Battalion 900/148.<br>– Elements of Battalion 900/148.<br>– <u>From Laos</u>: Three infantry battalions (910/148, 920/148, 970/176).<br>– <u>From the PRC</u>: One flak regiment (67 x 37mm AA guns).<br>(PLA advisers were already deployed extensively within the PAVN AA units at Dien Bien Phu) |
| | Initial French request made to US to provide personal body armour for the garrison. | US forces in Japan processed this request within 5 days. First drop made 8 days later (but landed with the Viet Minh!) First successful drops on 27 Apr (200 flak jackets to main position, 100 to Isabelle). Body armour had been readily available ever since the Korean conflict and its issue to the garrison before mid-Mar would undoubtedly have saved very many lives and injuries, and would to some extent have compensated for the inadequately constructed positions. |
| 14/15 Apr | Combined elements of 1 BEP and 2 BEP carried out night re-supply of ammunition and water to Huguette 6 (Captain Bizard) by 0240. Attacks launched by 1/13 DBLE(-) and 8 BPC(-) to cover their withdrawal by 1615. | |
| 15 Apr | French air supply drops achieved the maximum daily tonnage during the battle (250 tons, of which about 15 per cent was lost to the Viet Minh). | The same day, at 1700, a case fell from a French fighter-bomber into Viet Minh hands. It contained the latest map coverage, air photos, and details of all the French positions, targets and codes, plus the assessed communist locations. |
| | The Viet Minh launched an attack against sub-position Wieme (at Isabelle), just as an *ad hoc* force of T'ai troops was in the process of relieving the T'ai auxiliaries (commanded by Lieutenant Wieme) who had held the strong-point ever since the establishment of Isabelle.[29] | Regular Viet Minh attacks against Wieme continued, but with limited success. French counter-attacks to safeguard Wieme or to clear communist troops from its immediate area achieved varying results, but they did prevent the position being overrun. |
| 16 Apr | Hanoi advised the following promotions:<br>Colonel de Castries to brigadier general.<br>Lieutenant Colonel Langlais to colonel.<br>Lieutenant Colonel Lalande to colonel.<br>Major Bigeard to lieutenant colonel.<br>All captains commanding battalions to major. | De Castries' situation and promotion to general officer rank recalls Hitler's promotion of General Paulus, commander of the German Sixth Army, to field marshal shortly before his army's surrender at Stalingrad in February 1943. |
| 17–18 Apr | Decision taken (16 Apr) to evacuate Huguette 6 night 17/18 Apr. At 2000 Bigeard committed 1 BEP(-), 1/2 REI(-), 8 BPC and two M-24s to effect the withdrawal. The attack was halted by 2200 when it encountered strong Viet Minh bunker positions, and 1/4 RTM(-) and 6 BPC(-) were also committed; but by dawn on 18 Apr (Easter Sunday) the force was still in the area of Opéra and unable to reach Huguette 6. | Bigeard advised Captain Bizard that he could try to break out (without his wounded) or surrender if he wished. At 0800 the remaining legionnaires and paratroopers assaulted straight over the Viet Minh trenches and onwards across the open airfield. Remarkably, a number survived and reached Huguette 1 at 1040. Of those who had taken part in the defence of Huguette 6, 106 had died, 49 were wounded and 79 men were missing. Captain Bizard had led the spirited break-out and had survived unscathed. |

| Date | Summary of Event or Action | Remarks |
|------|---------------------------|---------|
| 19–23 Apr | Continued fierce fighting about the Huguette and Dominique positions, with Huguette 1 relieved by 1/13 DBLE(-) after a 14-hour battle on 19 Apr and a successful raid by 2/1 RCP(-) on the area of Dominique 2 and 5 during the night of 20/21 Apr. But at 0700 on 23 Apr Huguette 1 finally fell after a last stand by its 13 DBLE(-) legionnaires. | The loss of Huguette 1 on 23 Apr meant that virtually the whole airstrip was dominated by Viet Minh fire, which in turn further compromised the parachute drops of personnel or stores by reducing the DZ significantly. On the afternoon of 23 Apr, 2 BEP (with extensive combat air and artillery support, plus the last three M-24s) attempted to recapture Huguette 1. Although the attack inflicted significant casualties on the Viet Minh, it eventually failed due to a series of avoidable errors, with 150 French casualties sustained. As a result, the commanding officer of 2 BEP, Major Liesenfelt, was relieved of his command by Bigeard. He was replaced by Major Maurice Guiraud. 2 BEP(-) was amalgamated with 1 BEP(-) to form a composite 'Bataillon de Marche'. |
| 20–27 Apr | At Isabelle and Wieme the communist artillery bombardment and infantry attacks by PAVN Regiment No. 57 continued; as did the French counter-attacks. By the end of Apr most of the strongpoint – Wieme especially – was permanently inundated by the constant monsoon rainfall. The progressive and systematic destruction of the French emplacements by the communist artillery (including direct fire from 75mm recoilless rifles) meant that the protection against both fire and weather diminished daily. On 29 Apr only one M-24 was left fully operational. Thereafter, the fate of Isabelle converged with that of the main position, once the communists began their general offensive at the beginning of May. | As at 1400 on 20 Apr, Isabelle's original garrison of 1,809 men, three M-24s and eleven 105mm guns had been reduced to about 1,400 effectives, with two M-24s and eight guns. 117 men were severely wounded but could not be evacuated, and 136 were dead or missing. The declining morale of some of the Algerians in particular was exemplified by a failed (due to faulty intelligence) 2/1 RTA (commanded by Captain Pierre Jeancenelle) counter-attack on 26 Apr, following which Colonel Lalande ordered two men per platoon to be shot for cowardice at 1800 that evening. Fortunately for all involved, Lieutenant Cheik Belabiche, a company commander of 2/1 RTA, reasoned with Lalande, who compromised by ordering a formal (if somewhat surreal) court-martial of the Algerian soldiers, prior to which it had been agreed that they would all be found 'not guilty'! |

By nightfall on 23 April the often intense fighting that had ebbed and flowed about, into and within the Huguette positions for a week had reduced in tempo and died away, as both sides once again took stock of their respective situations.

Although the French positions had quite clearly been further substantially reduced since the first week of April, and the French Union forces had suffered some 500 casualties during that month alone, the Viet Minh losses had also been very heavy: totalling a number that was broadly equivalent to three full regiments of infantry. While many units of the French Union garrison had maintained their ability – against all the odds – to carry out offensive action, General Giap was very well aware that in the ranks of the PAVN the sheer scale of casualties suffered, together with the privations, problematical *matériel* support and often rudimentary medical arrangements available, were beginning to have a potentially disastrous effect upon the morale and combat effectiveness of many individual Viet Minh soldiers and their units. Again Giap recognised the time had come for a pause in his own offensives, to reinforce, replenish and prepare for what he knew must be the final, decisive attack.

On 22 April the full force of the tropical monsoon had deluged the valley, when many of the already permanently waterlogged emplacements were completely flooded and finally rendered unusable. Time was neither on the French side, nor that of the Viet Minh, as the battle entered the final week of April 1954 and the beleaguered garrison prepared itself for what it knew would be the decisive clash of arms. Failing massive reinforcement or American intervention, de Castries, Langlais, Bigeard, and Lalande[30] knew that they would have only those troops who were already in place to counter the impending communist onslaught on the French Union garrison of Dien Bien Phu.

As the thousands of troops at Dien Bien Phu once more prepared for combat, their senior commanders anxiously watched the rain-laden skies above the valley. For the French those skies offered a last hope of salvation, while for Giap they could yet prove to be the element that would frustrate all that he and the Viet Minh had achieved in Indo-China so far. However, as May Day 1954 approached, no significant change in the now spasmodic pattern of French air support was discernible.

**Table 21 – ORGANISATION AND DEPLOYMENT OF FRENCH FORCES 24 APRIL 1954**

| Location | Unit(s) | Local Commander | Personnel | Remarks |
|---|---|---|---|---|
| Claudine | 1/2 REI | Major Clémonçon | 400 | |
| | 3/1 RCC (-) | Lieutenant Adenot | | Captain Hervouët had been wounded on 31 Mar. |
| Huguette | 1 BEP/2 BEP (a composite battalion) | Captain Vieulles | 600 | Major Guiraud had been wounded 2 Apr, although he retained command of the northern sector of the main position. |
| | 1/ 4 RTM | | 140 | One company. |
| Junon | T'ai Company No. 414(-), plus French air force personnel | Captain Duluat | 180 | An *ad hoc* composite force. |
| Lily | 1/ 4 RTM(-) | Major Nicolas | 250 | |
| Eliane (part of) | 2/2 RCP 5 BPVN(-) 6 BPC(-) 1/13 DBLE(-) | Major Bréchignac | 1150 | Including overall command of the five hills about which the 'Battle of Les Paras' had raged at the beginning of Apr. |
| Eliane (part of) and Dominique 3 | 2 BT(-) 3/3 RTA(-) 6 BPC(-) | Major Chenel | 650 | Including overall command of the area of low ground east of the Nam-Youm. |
| Épervier and Opéra | 2 BT 5 BPVN 8 BPC Plus remaining quad-.50 heavy machine-guns | Major Tourret | 530 | One company. One company. |
| Isabelle | 2/1 RTA 5/7 RTA(-) 3 BT(-) 3/3 REI | Colonel Lalande | 1400 | One company. |
| | 3/1 RCC(-) | Lieutenant Henri Préaud | | One tank platoon(-). |

**Notes:** The command structure obtaining in the final three weeks of the battle was established after 10 April, when Langlais reorganised the garrison's command and defensive arrangements to be exclusively in the hands of the paratroop officers he knew and trusted. From this point, de Castries (and several other fairly senior but non-paratroop officers of the garrison) performed few if any command functions at Dien Bien Phu; although de Castries undoubtedly performed a useful service by continuing to deal on Langlais' behalf with the high command in Hanoi, thereby shielding Langlais and Bigeard from what would have been a time-consuming, frustrating and potentially acrimonious chore for these two tactical commanders. In addition to the command responsibilities indicated above, Major Michel Vadot (formerly chief of staff to Colonel Gaucher, who had been killed on 13 March) assumed overall command of the southern and western sectors. Bigeard became *de facto* Langlais' deputy, while retaining specific responsibility for counter-attacks. In April, the surviving elements of several of the above units and companies were re-grouped and re-named as 'Compagnies de Marche' or re-formed into other *ad hoc* groups to match the local tactical circumstances; the details of these tactical groupings of companies and part-units is beyond the scope of this work.

# INTERNATIONAL DIMENSIONS AND OTHER OPTIONS

For almost six months, apart from some more recent moves to convene an international conference in Geneva to resolve the conflict, the events at Dien Bien Phu had so far been an exclusively French affair.[31] It should be remembered that until only a few months before the first French Union airborne forces were launched into the Dien Bien Phu valley in November 1953, another war had been raging in nearby Korea. And certainly in Washington's eyes the progress and outcome of the conflicts in Indo-China and in Korea – both of which involved Western powers fighting against communist enemies – were inextricably linked. The rationale for this was the not illogical view that if either the US high command in Korea or that of the French in Indo-China negotiated a cease-fire in their own theatre of operations, the full weight of the communist forces thus released would be diverted to the other conflict. Ironically, the enforcement of this US foreign policy forestalled early moves by the French to negotiate with the Viet Minh while the Korean War was in full spate; the offset for which was an increase in US funding and *matériel* support for the campaign in Indo-China.

In mid-1953, however, the newly elected US President Dwight D. Eisenhower arbitrarily abrogated this declared policy, when he actively pursued his pre-election promise made to the American electorate by actively seeking and achieving a cease-fire in Korea. The US administration was well aware of the risk of this action, but considered at the time that France could deal with the increased military threat in Indo-China. But as 1953 moved to its close, this conveniently over-optimistic assessment[32] proved to be fatally flawed. Predictably, the price of Eisenhower's meeting his domestic obligations was an intensification of the Viet Minh campaign in Indo-China, as large quantities of artillery guns, ammunition, and all manner of *matériel* from China began to flood into Tonkin from the end of 1953. Just as significantly, this *matériel* was accompanied by hundreds of PLA advisers, fresh from their recent experience of fighting the US and other UN forces on the battlefields of Korea. Of particular value to the Viet Minh was the expertise of these advisers in the areas of artillery, logistics and air defence which had an almost immediate impact on the battle then developing at Dien Bien Phu. Furthermore, after mid-1953, the French campaign was conducted against the possibility of the communist Chinese air force – by now battle-experienced and with numbers of squadrons equipped with MiG-15 jet fighters – entering the conflict in support of the Viet Minh.

## Operation 'Damocles'

From the late autumn of 1953 the Washington administration encouraged the French war effort in *matériel* and financial terms, while distancing itself from direct involvement in Indo-China. Despite this, a contingency plan – Operation

'Damocles' – was developed, which would have involved a general French withdrawal southwards towards the Red River delta, pending the intervention of the ground forces of other nations and of US air-power. Clearly, the planners of 'Damocles' had in mind the Western response to a general communist Chinese intervention and its concept drew heavily upon the Korean experience. Nevertheless, although the extreme strategic scenario envisaged by the US planners was never judged to have developed, the rapidly deteriorating French situation necessary to trigger 'Damocles' had probably been more or less achieved by mid-March 1954. But in practice only clear evidence of direct Chinese intervention could have allowed the US to enter the conflict. For the French (while the military commanders at Dien Bien Phu would undoubtedly have welcomed US military intervention) in Paris Prime Minister Joseph Laniel was torn between the growing knowledge that, while only such an intervention could save Dien Bien Phu, at the same time it might well precipitate either the failure of the impending Geneva Conference – due to start on 26 April 1954 – or the entry of the People's Republic of China into the conflict: and in a worst case, possibly

Below: A French Union Infantryman takes cover as Viet Minh shells land on the airstrip. The amount and effectiveness of the communist artillery were badly underestimated by the French high command.

both outcomes would obtain. While the French considered and weighed their fast-diminishing political and military options, contingency planning for a possible US military air strike continued apace in Washington.

## Operation 'Vulture'

The planned air attack was code-named Operation 'Vulture', and it received serious consideration in Washington, notwithstanding the assessment that it would undoubtedly provoke direct armed intervention by the Chinese; which would in turn necessitate the direct air attack of targets in China. This subsequent phase would quite possibly include use of atomic weapons. The plan envisaged as many as 450 fighters and up to ninety-eight B-29 bombers involved in a first-strike that would deliver almost 1,400 tons of conventional bombs on to the Viet Minh about Dien Bien Phu. Follow-on missions would then be mounted as required to ensure the garrison's safety. The plan attracted considerable debate when it was briefed to a carefully selected audience at the US Department of State by Admiral Arthur B. Radford on 3 April 1954. At a later meeting in Paris on

14 April, US Secretary of State John Foster Dulles apparently expanded upon the original scope of 'Vulture', when he indicated the possibility of using two atomic bombs against the main Viet Minh positions in the Dien Bien Phu valley.[33]

The details of the ebb and flow of negotiation, political manoeuvring and planning that surrounded the question of US intervention in Indo-China in April 1954 is beyond the intended scope of this account of the battle. But it is generally true to say that in principle the US navy and air force both favoured intervention, while the army (foreseeing its commit-tal to another open-ended ground war in South-East Asia) did not. But the detail of these negotiations actually mattered not, because the eventual fate of 'Vulture' was actually settled at the 3 April meeting, when the senior members of Congress stipulated that US intervention would be unacceptable unless it were as part of a coalition that included the other non-communist nations of the region, including the Philippines, and – most significantly – the British Commonwealth.[34]

Although the concept of intervention was subsequently fully developed by an Anglo-US military planning team, the insistence of the US Congress that Great Britain would have to participate fully in the operation and that France would as soon as practicable thereafter be required to grant Indo-China full independence, were conditions unacceptable to the British and French governments. In addition to British government fears that any US intervention would certainly jeopardise the impending Geneva Conference on the future of Korea and Indo-China, Prime Minister Winston Churchill expressed his concern that a war with China would inevitably involve the Soviet Union, because of the Sino-Soviet Pact; which in turn could result in a Soviet nuclear attack on US air bases in Great Britain. This view expressed by one of the great leaders of the Second World War echoed many of those expressed during the recently ended Korean conflict, and added substance to the argument that communism should be contained by carefully controlled limited wars, rather than by attempting its defeat through total war. In any event, as the Operation 'Vulture' conditions imposed by the US Congress could not be agreed (Churchill indicated to Parliament in London on 27 April that any British military involvement in Indo-China prior to the Geneva Conference was unacceptable), and a growing number of practical operational difficulties were being identified by the American air force planners, President Eisenhower finally ruled against US military support for the French through the implementation of Operation 'Vulture'. The last act in the saga was a high-level meeting chaired by the President in Washington on 29 April, which also ruled out any unilateral military action by the United States. Thus was the fate of the garrison at Dien Bien Phu finally sealed, together with that of French Indo-China.

As a tail-piece to the ill-fated saga of 'Vulture', the often quite surreal nature of the whole business was exemplified by an event that took place in late April 1954. On 23 April, with the fate of Dien Bien Phu hanging in the balance, the French Under-Secretary of State André Bougenot, in the presence of the Prime Minister Laniel, once again approached Washington to seek US air support for the beleaguered French Union garrison. Somewhat bizarrely, he suggested that the United States 'could commit its naval aircraft to the battle of Dien Bien Phu without risking American prestige or committing an act of belligerency by placing such aircraft, painted with French insignia and construed as part of the French Foreign Legion, under nominal French command for an isolated action consisting of air strikes lasting two or three days'.[35] The French air force certainly did not have sufficient aircrew qualified in multi-engine aircraft to carry out the mission themselves, even if the aircraft had been provided. Meanwhile, the fact that such a pragmatic but diplomatically improbable solution had been seriously considered gained credibility with reports that USAF B-29 bombers had been observed at Clark USAF base in the Philippines with the blue, white and red French roundels already painted on them. However, this proposal suffered the same fate as all the others that involved international military intervention to save Dien Bien Phu.

## Operation 'Condor'

At the end of the first week of April, as the situation in the Dien Bien Phu valley became ever more acute and the likelihood of massive US military intervention receded, the French high command began to consider other options to aid the embattled garrison. As early as December 1953 General Navarre had initiated the planning for a complementary operation to be launched from Laos towards Dien Bien Phu with a view to exploiting what had then been assumed would be a French victory by completing the presumed rout of the Viet Minh forces besieging the French Union forces. This four-phase operation had been code-named Operation 'Condor'. It called for the involvement of some 5,500 troops, including airborne units, artillery and engineers; but most importantly it required a level of air transport support roughly equivalent to that which the original airborne force that dropped into Dien Bien Phu in November 1953 had needed. As such, the original plan for 'Condor' was unsustainable. But by early April 1954 it was abundantly clear to General Navarre and his staff that they could not rely upon US intervention to save Dien Bien Phu, and that alternative options were now urgently required.

Consequently, the 'Condor' plan was drastically modified and changed into an expedition launched from Laos with a view to alleviating the pressure on Dien Phu and achieving a physical link-up with the garrison in the area of Isabelle. The new plan was in all but name a military relief expedition in the traditional mould. The officer responsible for producing the new plan and overseeing the operation was Colonel Boucher de Crèvecoeur, commander of the French Union forces in Laos. The 'Condor' ground force comprised four battalions, which were further divided into two combat groups within Groupement Mobile Nord (GMN) commanded by Lieutenant Colonel Godard, and a separate Commando Group under the command of Lieutenant Colonel Mollat. The entire force was under the command of Colonel Then. Two Vietnamese airborne battalions were included in the modified plan, but were not used (and are not included in the total of 3,088 men who did deploy).

Table 22 – FRENCH UNION FORCES ALLOCATED TO OPERATION 'CONDOR'

| Unit | Tactical Grouping or Role | Commander | Remarks |
|---|---|---|---|
| 2/2 REI<br>4 BCL<br>(4e Bataillon de Chasseurs Laotiens) | Sub-Group West | Lieutenant Colonel Godard | 1/2 REI was already at Dien Bien Phu (Claudine). |
| 1 BPL<br>(1er Bataillon de Parachutistes Laotiens)<br>5 BCL | Sub-Group East | Major Coquelet | |
| GC<br>(Groupement de Commandos) | Screen, reconnaissance and deception | Lieutenant Colonel Mollat<br>Sub-Group A: Lieutenant Mesnier<br>Sub-Group B: Lieutenant Vang Po<br>Sub-Group C: Sergent Marcellin | Comprised of 800 Laotian and Meo tribesmen. |

Table 22 – FRENCH UNION FORCES ALLOCATED TO OPERATION 'CONDOR' (continued)

| Unit | Tactical Grouping or Role | Commander | Remarks |
|---|---|---|---|
| GC 610 (Groupement de Commandos No. 610) | Strategic reconnaissance and intelligence acquisition | Captain Lousteau | Under the direct control of the French high command. |
| Miscellaneous small groups from diverse French Union units in Indo-China | Operational deception | | These parties were deliberately sacrificed in order to deceive the Viet Minh if killed or captured. They were airlifted into the area in the firm belief that they were simply preceding the move of the remainder of their units. |
| 1 BPVN | Reserve and subsequent operations | | Available for the subsequent airborne phase, but not used. |
| 3 BPVN | Reserve and subsequent operations | | Available for the subsequent airborne phase, but not used. |
| GCMA (Groupement de Commandos Mixtes Aéroportés) (re-named 'Groupement Mixte d'Intervention' (GMI) from December 1953) | Strategic operations (as directed by the French high command), including the securing of the DZ for the (airborne) Phase 2 of Operation 'Condor' | Lieutenant Colonel Roger Trinquier | Not formally a part of Phase 1 of Operation 'Condor', but became increasingly involved with it indirectly as its ground force operated within their area north of the Nam Ou River. |

Despite extremely hot weather, and the fact that even during the monsoon the operational area was notoriously arid, both sub-groups moving separately achieved a number of tactical successes as they edged slowly northwards towards Dien Bien Phu during the last two weeks of April. Certainly the Viet Minh were aware of their presence and probable mission, and the threat that it might pose. On 29 April both sub-groups linked up on the Nam Ou River at Muong Khoua, less than eighty kilometres south-west of strong-point Isabelle. Here they hoped to draw Viet Minh forces away from Dien Bien Phu and, having fixed those forces on the banks of the Nam Ou, the 'Condor' force – four battalions strong – would move out to the east, circumvent the Viet Minh forces and reach Isabelle by the last week of May. Meanwhile, a GAP would be dropped to the north-east to reinforce 'Condor' force for the final advance across the Laos–Vietnam border and on to Dien Bien Phu. On that very day, Thursday 29 April, however, General Navarre informed Colonel de Crèvecoeur that the air transport necessary to execute phase two of 'Condor' had to be re-allocated to support Dien Bien Phu, where bad weather had seriously curtailed air supply operations. The air transport situation had also been considerably exacerbated by the American civilian aircrews' refusal on 24 April to continue flying their C-119 cargo aircraft into Dien Bien Phu, in light of the virtual wall of communist flak that by now greeted every sortie. The numbers of Viet Minh anti-aircraft 37mm and .50cal heavy machine-guns about Dien Bien Phu had increased appreciably during April, as had the weight of 105mm artillery fire falling on the garrison. With the GAP now not available to 'Condor' for at least a week, a critical element of the operation had been written out, and the whole concept of the mission designed to relieve Dien Bien Phu had to be changed once again.

The entire force now concentrated in defensive positions on the north side of the Nam Ou, and 'Condor' was re-named Operation 'Ariège'. The troops of 5 BCL had already pushed some kilometres north-east of the river and since 27 April had been engaged in a running fight with elements of PAVN Regiment No. 148. Screened by commandos of the GCMA, however, 5 BCL managed to break contact and withdrew to the river under cover of darkness on the night of 3 May. Unable to render any further assistance to Dien Bien Phu, and with the knowledge that a French defeat in the valley would release thousands of Viet Minh troops to join the battle against them, the force remained in place for five days. On the fifth day, 8 May, they heard that Dien Bien Phu had fallen, which was quickly followed by the receipt of orders to withdraw the entire force from the Nam Ou to the air-head at Muong Sai, almost 100 kilometres to the south. Of a necessity, this withdrawal was to be carried out unsupported, un-reinforced and at best speed. As the units began to pull out, the first widespread contacts with communist forces were reported by the forward positions. However, by and large the with-drawal was conducted successfully. This was due primarily to the professional competence of Lieutenant Colonel Godard – who deliberately moved his battalions along newly cut trails instead of the routes they had used on the move to the Nam Ou, and thereby pre-empted a comprehensive ambush laid by the Viet Minh – and the bravery of 5 RCL whose troops provided a rear-guard. Godard had also ordered the withdrawal routes to be mined, a number of these explosive devices being timed to explode at ten-minute intervals in order to frustrate any immediate pursuit. During the 'Ariège' withdrawal only 4 BCL sustained serious casualties, losing some 50 per cent of its effectives in a violent night battle on 8/9 May with the Viet Minh force that had been dispatched to ambush the withdrawing French troops. Despite the failure of 'Condor' – attributable in no way to the units deployed to carry it out – the French Union force eventually reached the safety of Muong Sai relatively unscathed, apart from 4 BCL.[36] With the demise of Operation 'Condor' on 29 April the last chance to save Dien Bien Phu by outside intervention had gone, but by the end of Operation 'Ariège' the whole rationale for 'Condor' had in any case also disappeared.

# 11
# PRELUDE TO DEFEAT
## 24–30 APRIL

With Operation 'Vulture' a non-starter and Operation 'Condor' effectively terminated, the final countdown had begun for Dien Bien Phu; although neither its courageous garrison nor the Viet Minh troops that surrounded it could yet be certain of this. Had General Giap known all that had transpired between Washington, London and Paris earlier in April, he might perhaps have been more confident of the outcome, in the knowledge that direct military intervention by the United States to save the French was no longer an option. In hindsight it may seem incredible that the Viet Minh should by late April have been anything other than buoyant and confident of victory; nevertheless the Viet Minh commanders were aware that the morale of many of their soldiers and junior commanders was by now anything but good, and the battle fatigue and huge losses they had incurred during almost six months of fighting had told on them to a very considerable extent.

By this stage many of the French soldiers would no doubt have known something of the possibility of Operations 'Vulture' or 'Condor' alleviating their situation, and have been heartened by this. But the balance of forces at Dien Bien Phu still showed that even with these tentative and risky operations in prospect the garrison's situation was dire, because General Giap had at his command about ten combat soldiers for every one that de Castries, Langlais and Bigeard could commit to battle. By late April the communist forces about Dien Bien Phu included some 35,000 infantrymen, supported by thousands of artillerymen, engineers, communications and logistic troops. In all, the PAVN forces at Dien Bien Phu equated to five divisions.

As April drew to a close, although the paper strength of the French Union garrison was still some 15,000 men (which was in reality no more than 4 per cent of the total French Union forces then in Indo-China), on 24 April there were in reality about 3,250 effective troops at the main position, and a further 1,400 at Isabelle. The assessment of 'combat effectiveness' was that made by Langlais and duly reported back to Hanoi by de Castries. It reflected motivation, *esprit de corps* and individual fighting spirit rather than actual physical condition, because many of these men

Right: Planning conference of the principal French Union parachute commanders at Dien Bien Phu in late April 1954. From left to right: Botella (5 BPVN), Gigeard (6 PBC), Tourret (8 BPC), Langlais (GAP 1), de Séguin-Pazzis (de Castries' chief of staff).

had already sustained severe injuries, but were ready to fight on. Meanwhile, beneath the main defensive position in the waterlogged tunnels and underground bunkers of Major Paul Grauwin's field hospital lay some 878 very severely wounded, and 117 in the hospital bunkers at Isabelle. Aggravated by the communist artillery fire and almost incessant rainfall, the conditions necessarily endured by the French wounded were appalling, despite the almost superhuman efforts of Major Grauwin and his medical assistants and auxiliaries. All of these wounded men would, in normal circumstances, have been evacuated from Dien Bien Phu by air long before.

Each day was now characterised by the insidious progress of the communist trench-diggers, as they gradually drove their tentacle-like excavations ever deeper into the original site of Dien Bien Phu. In places these entrenchments and tunnels passed beneath positions occupied by the French. On Saturday 24 April one such encroachment forced the evacuation of strong-point Opéra by the 5 BPVN company then manning it, before the small force of Vietnamese paratroopers became outflanked and cut off. From time to time the French units – usually with the paratroopers and Foreign Legion to the fore – mounted local counter-attacks, many of which regained a trench here, a bunker there. Other attacks were launched to destroy individual Viet Minh gun positions and bunkers, although new ones appeared almost daily as the ring of steel around the garrison tightened inexorably. As the perimeter shrank so the garrison noted an ever-increasing build-up of enemy strength to the east of the perimeter, and it became more and more difficult for the air-dropped supplies and reinforcements to be delivered with any degree of accuracy. Quantities did still land within or close enough to the French positions to be recovered, but much of the *matériel* landed among the Viet Minh and was subsequently used against the garrison.

One particularly welcome load did arrive safely on Tuesday 27 April, when 200 sets of body armour – 'flak jackets' – arrived at the main position and 100 at Isabelle. Had these arrived prior to 13 March they would undoubtedly have saved many lives, especially those of the artillerymen and mortarmen who had been required to serve their weapons in open pits throughout the battle. Many guns and mortars had already outlasted several of their crews, but by 27 April only one of the four original 155mm medium howitzers remained fully operational.

On Wednesday 28 April the monsoon weather prevented any air drops on to the main position, though some personnel and stores did arrive at Isabelle. At 2200 that evening the French paratroopers at Huguette carried out a raid on the communist trenches a few hundred metres to their front, and killed more than twenty Viet Minh while sustaining only three wounded among their own number.

By dawn on Thursday 29 April almost all the French positions were one metre deep in mud, following an entire night of rain, which had also inhibited the night supply drop. The supply situation – already critical following the destruction by shellfire of a ration dump three days earlier – was further aggravated by a storm of artillery fire which fell across the main position that morning, destroying a dump of 600 rounds of artillery ammunition. As the bombardment continued, a number of new Viet Minh 75mm and 105mm artillery positions, all ranged against the eastern positions, were noted as the build-up continued. That night, a 105mm shell hit the hull of one of the two remaining M-24 tanks at the main position. It was dragged away to one of the Huguette positions so that its still serviceable 75mm gun and turret machine-guns could be employed as a fixed fire position.

On 29 April the nurse Lieutenant Geneviève de Galard-Terraube was summoned to the GAP 2 command post at 1800 hours. For a full month she had been working alongside Major Grauwin in the underground hospital, the only French woman serving at Dien Bien Phu. When she entered the command post, de Castries stepped forward and formally announced her award of the Croix de Guerre with Palms, and her appointment as a Chevalier of the Légion d'honneur. For this ceremony the appropriate medal and cross were borrowed from a lieutenant and from Langlais respectively, and her well-deserved awards were universally applauded by the garrison. For those involved, this ceremony also provided an all too brief period of normality in circumstances that were in every other respect anything but normal.

The efforts made by a number of the élite units of the French garrison to maintain the traditions normally observed in usually less acute situations continued next day, for Friday 30 April was Camerone Day. On this day each year the Legion commemorates the gallantry of the three officers and sixty-two NCOs and legionnaires of the 3rd Company, 1st Battalion of the Foreign Legion Regiment who had fought almost to the last man against a vastly superior Mexican force at the hamlet of Camerone on 30 April 1863.[37] No doubt many of the legionnaires who heard the traditional reading of the account of the battle that day were able to empathise more closely than usual with their forebears of almost a century earlier.

At Dien Bien Phu, that Camerone Day in 1954 was also notable for several more immediate reasons. First and foremost, on that Friday the American civilian aircrews who flew the C-119 cargo aircraft, but who had refused to do so since 24 April, resumed flying — but at a height that reduced the threat posed by anti-aircraft fire. This of course reduced the accuracy of the drops significantly, with 30–50 per cent of each load falling into Viet Minh hands, or into areas comprehensively covered by their observed fire. But the (approximately) 2,500 legionnaires at Dien Bien Phu may well have viewed the resumption of the C-119 supply drops as a welcome present on the Foreign Legion's most important day of the year. Most appropriately and in the best tradition of the Legion, a sortie that night by soldiers of the 1/13 DBLE from Eliane destroyed a Viet Minh bunker and killed at least ten communist soldiers. This sortie also recovered two containers of 'Vinogel' (wine concentrate) which had been air-dropped but fallen into the area adjacent to the Viet Minh bunker… the principal purpose of the operation! For a legionnaire, Camerone Day without any alcohol at all was unthinkable, so long as there was even the most remote chance of procuring it! The operational situation notwithstanding, in accordance with Foreign Legion tradition, at a ceremony conducted by Lieutenant Colonel Lemeunier at the command bunker of the 13 DBLE, several non-legion personnel of the garrison were made 'honorary legionnaires'. On Camerone Day at Dien Bien Phu those so honoured included de Castries, Langlais, Bigeard and Geneviève de Galard-Terraube.

Meanwhile, all about the perimeter of the French positions, patrol activity, limited sorties and skirmishes continued, as the Viet Minh edged their trenches ever deeper into Dien Bien Phu. That aspect of 30 April was no different from any other day in the valley since mid-March: the men of both sides continued to fight and die at one another's hands. But as April turned to May, despite the very many casualties and extensive *matériel* losses that the communists had suffered at the hands of the French air force on the logistic lines of communication to Dien Bien Phu, General Giap's build-up was at last complete, and a huge assault force now lay in concentration areas not far from the eastern perimeter of the main French position.

Although the French air force had continued dropping individual reinforcements into Dien Bien Phu in parallel with its other supply drops right up to and even during the final battle, the fate of Dien Bien Phu was no longer in any doubt.

**The Last Days, 1–6 May**

Coincidentally, the Legion's Camerone Day was immediately succeeded by May Day, annually celebrated and marked by socialists, communists, workers and labour movements throughout the world. Accordingly, on that morning of Saturday 1 May the Viet Minh positions all about Dien Bien Phu blossomed with many hundreds of red flags of all types and sizes, and suitably patriotic music blared out from loud-speakers positioned among the trenches and bunkers. Apart from an early morning counter-attack by paratroopers to recapture ground at position Huguette 5 and an overnight battle at Isabelle to regain French control of strong-point Wieme, the steady tempo of communist artillery and anti-aircraft fire and probing attacks that had persisted each day during the previous weeks was replaced by a general lull right across the battlefield. But although

Right: A French Union 105mm howitzer position. These open gun pits could be seen from the Viet Minh positions in the hills and proved very vulnerable to the communist artillery fire from mid-March 1954.

overt military action had diminished, the level of Viet Minh radio traffic and the redeployment of units and artillery pieces – often in full view of the garrison – increased significantly as the day wore on. For the almost 15,000[38] members of the garrison – though fewer than 5,000 could truly be categorised as combat troops, and of these fewer than 3,000 remained capable of carrying out any effective offensive action – it was abundantly clear that Giap's final attack was imminent. Although the French were now defending a much reduced area, they had only one-third the troop strength that had countered the Viet Minh

attacks of mid-March. The garrison's food supply was sufficient for three days, but they had less than twenty-four hours' worth of artillery and mortar ammunition with which to resist an assault that promised to be unprecedented in scale or tempo.

At 1700 hours the short respite ended, as hundreds of guns and mortars began their preliminary bombardment of the remaining French positions on Claudine, Huguette, Eliane, Dominique, Lily and Épervier. At first, the principal tactical commanders, now all commanding *ad hoc* and several times amalgamated units, in the main positions were: Major Clémençon and Captain Bienvault (Claudine), Major Guiraud (Huguette), Majors Bréchignac and Coutant (Eliane), Major Chenel (Dominique), Major Nicolas (Lily), Major Tourret and Captain Bizard (Épervier) and Captain Duluat (Junon). Colonel Langlais and Lieutenant Colonel Bigeard continued to fulfil their overall command and counterattack responsibilities, while Brigadier de Castries remained in overall titular command of the garrison. At Isabelle, Colonel Lalande continued to command that strong-point and strong-point Wieme.

At 2000 hours the first infantry assaults rolled towards Dominique and Eliane, as major elements of the 312th and 316th PAVN Divisions closed in from the east, and those of the 308th Division from the northwest. By about 0200 on 2 May Dominique 3 and Eliane 1 had fallen to the soldiers of the 312th and 316th Divisions, and the thirty men holding Huguette 5 had been overwhelmed by the 308th Division's assault. Further to the south, the 304th Division began its own attacks against Isabelle. As the rapidly deteriorating situation at Dien Bien Phu became clear in Hanoi, it at last prompted General Cogny to order

**Table 23 – FRENCH UNION REINFORCEMENTS PARACHUTED INTO DIEN BIEN PHU BETWEEN 24 APRIL AND 6 MAY 1954**

| Number of Reinforcements or Unit | Remarks |
|---|---|
| Seventy-two individual reinforcements | Dropped night 23/24 Apr. Included replacement crews for the M-24s. |
| Fifty-one individual reinforcements | Dropped 25 Apr. |
| Fifty individual reinforcements | Dropped 27 Apr. |
| Twenty-four individual reinforcements | Dropped at Isabelle 28 Apr (none dropped at the main position that day). All were Foreign Legion volunteers. |
| Forty-three individual reinforcements | Dropped 1 May. |
| 1 BPC(-) (1er Bataillon de Parachutistes Coloniaux) | Dropped (incomplete) at night between 3 and 5 May 54. 1 BPC was commanded by Captain Guy de Bazin de Bezon, who was seriously wounded on 5 May within hours of arriving at Dien Bien Phu, when Captain Jean Pouget assumed command of 1 BPC. |
| Ninety-one men of 1 BPC | Dropped 0412 – 0520, Thursday 6 May. These were the last reinforcements parachuted into Dien Bien Phu. Although the full strength of 1 BPC numbered 876 men, only 383 were successfully parachuted into Dien Bien Phu between 3 and 6 May. |

**Notes:** Between 13 March and 6 May 1954, a total of 4,291 reinforcements arrived at Dien Bien Phu. Of these, 3,507 personnel were in formed units; the remaining 784 personnel were individual reinforcements. A total of 680 volunteers who were not parachute-qualified were dropped (with very few parachuting-related injuries), and fourteen individual reinforcements were air-landed. From 1 May, a further 450 trained paratroopers were airlifted by USAF aircraft to Indo-China direct from the French parachute training centres at Pau and Vannes, but they did not arrive until 8 May, and so were not in time to be committed to the final battle.

The final reinforced strength of the garrison 'on paper' was 15,105 troops, although many of these were not by definition 'combat troops' – infantrymen, artillerymen or tank crewmen – and the 15,105 is a relatively unhelpful statistic for purposes of comparison. Of more use is Colonel Langlais' assessment that there were about 2,900 effective combat troops in the garrison as at 1 May. That said, any and all of the French Union troops of the garrison of necessity became 'combat troops' between 1 and 8 May. Similarly, not all the 35,000 Viet Minh ranged against the garrison were assault troops, and due to the heavy casualties incurred during the earlier battles the levels of training, morale and quality of very many of the communist soldiers who carried out the attacks of 1–8 May were very low, although this cannot be quantified with any accuracy.

At the time of the final battle, about 2,440 Viet Minh prisoners of war were being held within the garrison.

that 1 BPC, the sole remaining reserve airborne battalion in Indo-China, should be dropped to reinforce the garrison. Although this reinforcing action was partially accomplished by 6 May it was by then a case of too little, too late. Throughout 2 May the battle ebbed and flowed across and around the positions, but the garrison was no longer capable of mounting the spirited counter-attacks that had characterised the fighting during March and early April. Coincidentally, the provision of combat air support reached a crisis on 1 May, with the withdrawal of a complete carrier-based squadron due to the exhaustion of its pilots. The toll of aircrew had been very heavy, and for all categories of combat and observation aircraft and helicopters as at 2 May, the number of airframes now exceeded the crews available to man them. A refusal by French civilian cargo aircraft pilots to fly C-119 missions to Dien Bien Phu further aggravated the air support situation. Despite the more obvious perils of flying their missions, the C-47 flights continued, and the following day 107 reinforcements were successfully dropped into the garrison; although on that same day it lost some 420 men as battle casualties. Meanwhile, all across Dien Bien Phu the torrential monsoon rains fell upon French and communist soldiers alike, and turned the battlefield into a sea of mud, churned by explosions, Viet Minh tunnelling, collapsing earthworks, and the constant passage to and fro of thousands of fighting men.

The Monday night of 3/4 May was the night that Huguette 4 finally fell. Soon after midnight a force of more than 3,000 Viet Minh – some seven battalions supported by an artillery regiment – assaulted the position that was being held by Captain Jean Lucciani with about eighty legionnaires and Moroccan soldiers. The PAVN force was commanded overall by General Vuong Than Vu, command-ing general of the 308th Division. Although the French casualties increased steadily, those on the communist side were soon numbered in hundreds, most of whom lay in droves in front of the French trenches, many bodies being draped on the barbed wire. Remarkably, the French held on and at 0300 the Viet Minh attack faltered, as several of its regimental and battalion commanders who had failed thus far were replaced in the field. One French intelligence report indicated that the general commanding the attack may also have been removed. But the sheer weight of numbers eventually told, and half-an-hour later the Viet Minh broke into the last bunker: a fact reported by one of the last ten soldiers even as he died in a hail of bullets. Although Major Maurice Guiraud organised about 100 men and the remaining M-24 tank to mount a counter-attack at 0600 hours, this small force was up against more than 2,000 men and from the outset it was a gallant but hopeless venture. The counter-attack did reach the perimeter of the Huguette 4 defences before it was finally beaten back; testament not only to the determination and courage of those involved, but also another indication of the reduced morale and quality of the Viet Minh who had captured Huguette 4 but at very great cost. For the French forces involved, this fight had resulted in fourteen dead, fifty-eight wounded and

150 missing. The seriously wounded were taken to the underground hospital, where more than 1,200 of their comrades already lay. By dawn on 4 May Viet Minh troops were within 300 metres of de Castries' command bunker in several places and, even though the ordinary soldiers still clung to hopes of outside intervention, Brigadier de Castries and Colonel Langlais knew that the fall of Dien Bien Phu was now inevitable and imminent. By midnight on Tuesday 4 May the French artillerymen had fired during that day alone no less than forty 155mm shells, 1,180 of the 120mm mortar bombs and 2,600 of the shells for their 105mm howitzers: a rate of consumption that, if sustained, would probably exhaust the remaining stocks of artillery ammunition within thirty-six hours unless there was an immediate and dramatic increase in the quantity and accuracy of the air supply drops.

Wednesday 5 May dawned with the familiar torrents of falling rain, while wreaths of smoke and mist eddied across the battlefield. On, or more accurately beneath, the remaining legionnaires of the 1/13 DBLE on position Eliane 2, the Viet Minh were busily extending a tunnel that would be filled with explosives to

Below: The ten M-24 tanks deployed to Dien Bien Phu proved particularly effective at a tactical level, but they were too few in number to affect the wider battle.

blow away the strong-point. That same day a company of the newly arrived 1 BPC paratroops, commanded by Captain Jean Pouget (former aide-de-camp to General Navarre), relieved the 1/13 DBLE legionnaires on Eliane 2. The existence of the communist mineshaft was well-known, but the French troops derived a perverse comfort from the sound of the digging, which meant that it was not yet ready. Every member of a small patrol that the 1 BPC company later sent out in an attempt to destroy the mineshaft entrance died in a hail of gunfire without achieving their mission.

Meanwhile, as darkness once again fell over the battlefield, on Claudine five Moroccan soldiers of 1/4 RTM slipped away from their guard position, cut through the two lines of barbed wire which protected that part of Claudine, and deserted to the communists. The position had been manned by a mixed force of 1/4 RTM and 2/1 REI, and as soon as the desertion was discovered a group of legionnaires from 2/1 REI attempted to close the potentially disastrous gap in their barbed wire defences. But the Viet Minh had anticipated this reaction and had immediately and comprehensively covered the gap with fire; seven legionnaires died and twelve were wounded in the attempt. The remaining 2/1 REI legionnaires disarmed those Moroccans still at that part of Claudine, and ejected them from the position to survive as best they might among the many hundreds of 'internal deserters' that by now populated the banks of the Nam-Youm River at Dien Bien Phu.

By the end of 5 May, the garrison had sustained fourteen fatal casualties and forty-eight wounded. There were no reserves of combat troops left to deploy – every man still effective was in the line – and the remaining stocks of ammunition were dwindling fast. At 2100 Major General Cogny radioed Brigadier de Castries and authorised him to attempt to break out of the position if he decided that further resistance was hopeless. Unwelcome and unthinkable (given Navarre's concept of Dien Bien Phu) though it was, the possibility of a break-out had already been considered by the high command and by the senior commanders at Dien Bien Phu: particularly in the context of Operation 'Condor', when in more favourable circumstances a link-up between that force and at least some of those escaping the Viet Minh encirclement of Dien Bien Phu might have been feasible. But the demise of 'Condor' had put an end to that possibility, and so the urgent detailed planning from the night of 5 May for what was code-named Operation 'Albatros' was necessarily constrained to a concept that envisaged a desperate last-minute break-out: to be attempted only by those French Union soldiers whose physical condition still afforded them any hope of success. In the event, there would be no successful break-out from the main position, although that carried out from Isabelle did manage to achieve a small degree of success.

The night of 5/6 May saw one of the most sizeable drops of ammunition and *matériel* since mid-April. This was a consequence of slightly improved weather, and the return to duty of the French civilian pilots who had refused to fly these missions just three days earlier. Although the cargo drops were made, the weight

**Table 24 – ORGANISATION AND DEPLOYMENT OF FRENCH UNION COMBAT FORCES, THURSDAY 6 MAY 1954**

| Location (refer to map on p. 101) | Unit | Local Tactical Commanders | Remarks |
|---|---|---|---|
| Eliane 2 | 1 BPC (two companies) | Captain Pouget, Lieutenant Edme | |
| Eliane 3 | 1/13 DBLE(-)<br>1/4 RTM(-) | Captain Coutant | |
| Eliane 4 | 2/1 RCP(-)<br>5 BPVN(-)<br>1 BPC (two companies) | Major Bréchignac, Major Botella, Captain Tréhiou, Captain Penduff | |
| Eliane 10 and adjacent strongpoints | 6 BPC(-)<br>2 BT(-) | Major Thomas, Major Chenel, Captain Fazentieux | Plus a number of individual paratroopers, Algerian soldiers and combat engineers. |
| Junon | 1/13 DBLE(-)<br>Air force personnel, T'ai tribesmen and the section of Quad .50cal HMGs | Captain Charnod, Captain Duluat, Lieutenant Redon | The majority of the seriously wounded (in excess of 600) were also in Junon's emplacements. |
| Claudine | 1/2 REI(-)<br>1/13 DBLE(-) | Major Clémençon, Captain Coldeboeuf, Captain Hervouët | |
| Épervier and Dominique 4 | 8 BPC(-) | Major Tourret, Captain Bizard | |
| Lily | *Ad hoc* force of legionnaires and Moroccan troops | Major Nicolas | |
| Huguette 2 and 3 | Composite Foreign Legion Airborne Battalion (formed from remnants of 1 BEP and 2 BEP) (about 160 troops) | Major Guiraud | |
| Isabelle | 3/3 REI<br>2/1 RTA<br>5 RTA<br>3 BT(-) | Colonel Lalande | |

of anti-aircraft fire was such that the personnel drops were severely disrupted, and as dawn broke only ninety-one men of 1 BPC had dropped successfully – the last personnel to be dropped into Dien Bien Phu. The onset of daylight made the lumbering C-47s easy targets for the communist gunners, and so these aircraft turned away from the valley for the last time; with the bulk (493 paratroopers) of 1 BPC still aboard, and more awaiting their turn at the airbase near Hanoi. That morning also saw an almost unprecedented number of French air force combat aircraft – sixty-five fighters of various types, plus forty-seven B-26 bombers – appear above the valley and set about attacking the communist anti-aircraft positions with a will and no little success.

That day, the garrison successfully mounted some local counter-attacks which undoubtedly boosted morale. But the French commanders knew that the impact of these small victories was entirely transient; and more significantly they indicated that the communists had merely paused to re-group, replenish and balance their divisions for the final assault. Even at this late stage, the men who had thus far directed and commanded a successful but ill-conceived defensive operation against all the odds still believed that the garrison might be saved by external intervention. For them and for those they commanded, it was unthinkable that they would be abandoned, for they – much better than the politicians in Paris – understood that the fate of the French Union garrison at Dien Bien Phu was now bound inextricably to the fate of French Indo-China: to preserve which they and their predecessors had been fighting ever since 1945.

Below: After the airstrip became unusable, French Union reinforcements were parachuted into the beleaguered garrison until 6 May.

On Thursday 6 May the garrison still hoped – however forlorn that hope – and in many cases still believed that a political solution, international military or diplomatic intervention, the French air force, or even Operation 'Condor' (which de Castries and Langlais still believed was viable) would relieve their situation and mean that the French, Vietnamese, North African, Laotian and Foreign Legion lives lost during the previous six months had not been sacrificed in vain. Given all that they had endured, their faith in their military commanders in Hanoi, Saigon and Paris was remarkable; but it was in the best tradition of the soldiers of France, and of the regiments to which they belonged.

Beneath Eliane 2 the Viet Minh engineers had at last stopped excavating and had been replaced by a long line of civilian porters, who now laboured to place almost three tonnes of high explosive at the head of the 47-metres-long tunnel.

At Colonel Langlais' operational planning meeting late that morning, it was disclosed by Captain Noël, the principal intelligence staff officer, that the headquarters at Hanoi had learnt that General Giap had scheduled the final overwhelming assault to destroy Dien Bien Phu to begin that very evening – Thursday 6 May.

# 12

# THE FINAL ONSLAUGHT
## 6–8 MAY

Right: French Union trenches and bunkers at Dien Bien Phu. The level of protection they provided soon proved generally inadequate against the Viet Minh artillery fire.

At 1200 on Thursday 6 May, after a short period of relatively minor activity, a new noise was heard at Dien Bien Phu. This was the screaming whistle of the first of many salvos of Soviet-made Katyusha rockets roaring into the valley from their mobile launch vehicles. These weapons had been moved into position during the previous weeks and their unmasking on 6 May was a complete and shocking revelation to the French troops. During a period of several hours the high-explosive warheads of these missiles comprehensively destroyed many of the remaining trenches, bunkers, ammunition dumps and supply points throughout the garrison. From 1730 hours the 'conventional' Viet Minh artillery joined the Katyusha bombardment in preparation for the final assault. As usual, the Eliane positions bore the brunt of this bombardment, which clearly indicated where the first blow would fall.

At 1845 battle was joined on the slopes of Eliane, as more than 1,000 Viet Minh of the PAVN 308th Division's Infantry Regiment No. 102 – the 'Capital Regiment' – surged towards Eliane 2. The first assault wave was slaughtered by the French artillery, but communist counter-battery fire destroyed three of the remaining 105mm guns at the main position, leaving seven still operational; plus one 155mm gun. During the next few hours, the communist artillery also destroyed eight of the nine remaining 105mm guns at Isabelle, thereby ending the residual French artillery's capability to support the main position from that southern strong-point. Despite a partial withdrawal from Eliane 2 and areas of Claudine being overrun, a counter-attack by a mixed force of legionnaires had re-taken control of Claudine by about 2230, but with no further artillery support or hope of reinforcement this force was finally over-whelmed at 0200 next morning.

The assault against Eliane 4 and Eliane 10 was launched at 2200, and involved two regiments of Viet Minh troops from the 312th and 316th Divisions. Remarkably, this first attack was halted by the remnant of 5 BPVN. The focus next moved to the positions held by the remaining troops of 6 BPC, and by 0300 only one bunker was still in French hands. A possible drop of reinforcements of 1 BPC was proposed

during this action, but the idea was reluctantly abandoned, the higher priority being the need of flare illumination so that the French Union troops could continue to engage the Viet Minh. If the paratroopers had dropped on to the fully illuminated battlefield few if any would have survived. Their arrival would have done little to affect the outcome of the battle, and would simply have swelled the final casualty figures. Langlais and Bigeard continued to try to fight the battle and redeploy their forces to the hard-pressed Eliane positions, but their options were

now virtually non-existent, and the remaining cohesion of the defence was dissipating. Then, at 2300 hours, the Viet Minh at last detonated the enormous landmine which they had emplaced under Eliane 2.

The huge explosion assumed many of the characteristics of an earthquake or volcanic eruption as the shock wave and blast of fire and smoke rolled away from the seat of the detonation. The awesome destruction wrought by the mine's detonation virtually wiped out the company of paratroops that had been positioned almost immediately above it. But the shock effect impacted upon both sides, and the Viet Minh failed to overrun the position before the surviving defenders brought fire to bear upon the waves of attackers who now found the massive, muddy crater impeding their advance. Despite the potential advantage afforded the communists by the explosion, the position at Eliane 2 was still in French hands at about 0300 hours. The commander, Captain Pouget, who had so far conducted a heroic defence of Eliane 2, sought reinforcements in order to consolidate his success, but there were none to be had, and shortly after 0400 hours on the morning of 7 May his remaining thirty or so men finally succumbed to the sheer weight of numbers that the communist Infantry Regiment No 102 threw against Eliane 2. At about 0440 the last shots from Eliane 2 were fired from the machine-gun of the disabled M-24 tank which had been emplaced as a gun position, and the Viet Minh soldiers finally took control of the long-embattled Eliane 2.

Throughout the battle for Eliane 2, the defenders of Eliane 4 and Eliane 10 had managed to stem the tide of the Viet Minh assault. But shortly after 0800 hours on the damp and cloudy morning of Friday 7 May, General Giap launched a large element of the 308th Division against the remaining Eliane positions. Apart from a handful of paratroopers who fought on briefly from the command bunker area, Eliane 4 succumbed at about 0900. Eliane 10 also fell at about 0930 hours when Major Thomas' men and the few surviving soldiers of 6 BPC were at last overcome. Some of the Moroccan soldiers in positions adjacent to Eliane 10 tied their *chéchia* (white headdress) to their rifle barrels and waved these in token of surrender, and these last positions on the Elianes were finally overrun shortly after midday. At 1030 Major Tourret and Captain Bizard were ordered to withdraw from Épervier and take up a new position deeper within the rapidly shrinking perimeter. The only fire support that was still creating mayhem and slaughter on a grand scale among the close-packed ranks of Viet Minh assault troops were the quad .50cal heavy machine-guns, now virtually buried under the many thousands of empty cartridge cases that surrounded these very effective weapons. By mid-morning, even the Claudine positions were beginning to crumble as the communist onslaught continued unabated.

Brigadier de Castries reported the rapidly deteriorating situation to General Cogny in Hanoi, and outlined the garrison's plans for a break-out from Dien Bien Phu that night. Code-named Operation 'Albatros', this was the third of the three suggested options that had been studied in the hope of restoring, alleviating or

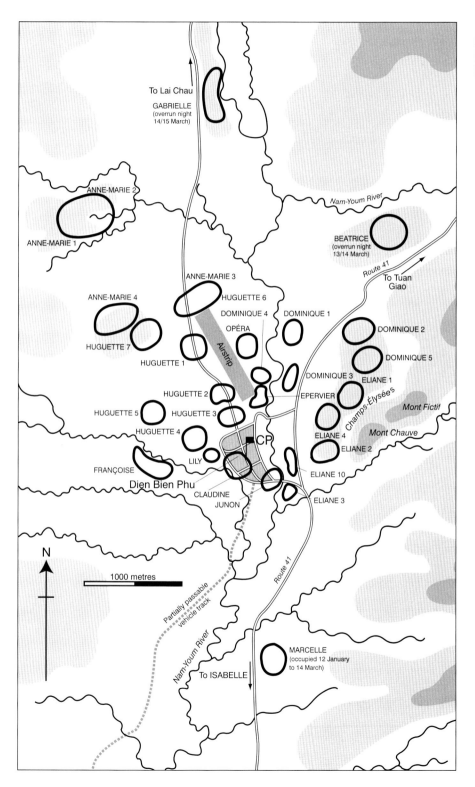

**FRENCH MAIN
DEFENSIVE
POSITION
MARCH – MAY
1954**

To Lai Chau

GABRIELLE
(overrun night
14/15 March)

ANNE-MARIE 2

ANNE-MARIE 1

Nam-Youm River

BEATRICE
(overrun night
13/14 March)

Route 41

To Tuan
Giao

ANNE-MARIE 3

ANNE-MARIE 4

HUGUETTE 6

DOMINIQUE 4

DOMINIQUE 1

OPÉRA

DOMINIQUE 2

HUGUETTE 7

DOMINIQUE 5

HUGUETTE 1

Airstrip

DOMINIQUE 3

ELIANE 1

HUGUETTE 2

EPERVIER

Champs-Élysées

Mont Fictif

HUGUETTE 5

HUGUETTE 3

HUGUETTE 4

Mont Chauve

CP

ELIANE 4

LILY

ELIANE 2

FRANÇOISE

Dien Bien Phu

ELIANE 10

CLAUDINE
JUNON

ELIANE 3

N

1000 metres

Partially passable
vehicle track

Route 41

Nam-Youm River

To ISABELLE

MARCELLE
(occupied 12 January
to 14 March)

salvaging the fortunes of the garrison at Dien Bien Phu. The first, 'Vulture', which posited large-scale air strikes by external forces, primarily the US Air Force, had been written-off because of political complications; the second, 'Condor', a relief expedition from Laos, failed; and now came 'Albatros' which was intended to save at least some of the garrison from death or capture, and – though this was not admitted – salvage a small element of French military pride from what was by 7 May an imminent and catastrophic defeat of French arms.

By the time that 'Albatros' was receiving serious consideration, the physical state of the garrison was such that the operation was no longer viable in its original form. The simple plan developed by Bigeard had called for all those still able

Right: French Union trenches close to the airstrip at Dien Bien Phu. Note the destroyed aircraft.

to march and fight to be split into two groups: one of paratroops (led by Bigeard) and one of non-paras (led by Major Vadot). At the chosen moment on the night of 7/8 May one group would strike out for the jungle-clad hills and mountains away to the west, and find safety some 100 kilometres beyond; the other would launch a final – certainly suicidal – attack eastwards to divert the communists' attention. The groups' respective roles were to be established by the two commanders drawing straws. It was understood that no wounded or otherwise non-combatant personnel could be involved in this venture, so their future as prisoners of war was already decided. Meanwhile, Colonel Lalande's troops at Isabelle would conduct their own break-out to the south. Langlais had approved

Below: From March 1954, the communist artillery fire made any movement above ground by day extremely hazardous.

the plan, but at a meeting of commanders late on the morning of 7 May it became all too clear that there were simply too few able-bodied troops still available to give it even a chance of success. This assessment was reinforced by new intelligence information, which showed quite clearly that three newly constructed Viet Minh trenches effectively barred the intended escape route from the valley. The command conference concluded at 1300 hours, by which time the assembly had decided that, with 'Albatros' a non-starter, a wholesale surrender politically and militarily unacceptable, and a fight to the finish unsupportable in humanitarian terms in view of the large numbers of wounded within Dien Bien Phu, Brigadier de Castries would be asked to declare a cease-fire at 1730 hours: thereby ending the fighting without a formal capitulation.

The niceties of this solution were no doubt lost on all but the high command and senior commanders in Hanoi, Saigon and Dien Bien Phu, and the French politicians; for nothing could disguise the fact of the impending Viet Minh victory

Below: Major Bigeard's use of the radio to organise, launch and co-ordinate decisive counter-attacks during the final months of the battle was masterful. Here Bigeard (seated) issues orders while conferring with Captain Botella of 5 BPVN (right).

and French defeat. For the French military, however, the imperative that no white flag be flown above Dien Bien Phu outweighed all other considerations, as the principal officers of the high command – notably Major General Cogny and General Navarre – contrived by any means, no matter how tenuous, to salvage at least some honour from the débâcle they had created some six months earlier. As for the soldiers at Dien Bien Phu, especially those who had fought throughout the siege and final battles, their gallantry and determination in the face of over-whelming odds certainly deserved better than a white flag at the end of it all, and so the solution arrived at by Langlais, Bigeard, Vadot and Lemeunier certainly reflected their knowledge and understanding of the nature and motivation of those under their direct command. At the same time it illustrated their awareness of the political implications of that which they proposed to de Castries.

Even as de Castries was considering Langlais' recommended course of action, any residual hope that some might escape from Dien Bien Phu vanished when, at 1500 hours, the communists resumed their attack from east and west. This action had been prompted by numbers of the Moroccan troops on Eliane 3 wav-ing white towels or their white headdresses while abandoning their positions and making towards the Viet Minh lines, which indicated to the Viet Minh high command that Dien Bien Phu was about to fall, and the consequent need of ensuring that the ring around the garrison be maintained as tightly as possible. At this time, many of the remaining T'ai troops began to discard their uniforms and put on civilian clothes.

It was now absolutely clear that no French Union soldier would be able to escape from the main position at Dien Bien Phu, and so de Castries agreed that at 1730 hours the French would cease firing.[39] He instructed his air support staff officer, Major Jacques Guérin, to cease all combat air support missions from 1700 hours, cancel all planned ammunition drops, and from 1600 to drop only food supplies.

At about 1600 the last of the French Union positions to the east of the Nam-Youm River were overrun by the Viet Minh. At 1700 de Castries provided a final update on the situation to Cogny in Hanoi, in a conversation that centred upon the white flag issue. The precise words used by de Castries at the end of his final transmission to Cogny vary slightly according to the source, the literal interpre-tation of the French, and further interpretation of the intended meaning of the words used. But the text quoted by the French press agency was probably correct and stated: 'The transmitter will be destroyed at 1730. We shall fight to the end.[40] *Au revoir mon Général, Vive la France!*' This was followed at 1730 by: 'I'm blow-ing up all the installations. The ammunition depots are already exploding. *Au revoir.*' Major General Cogny's reply was: 'Well then, *au revoir*, old boy.'

Seconds later a final message was transmitted from de Castries' secure radio link to Hanoi by a Sergent Millien, who reported: 'In five minutes, everything will be blowing up here. The Viets are only a few metres away. Greetings to every-body.' Thereafter, there was silence.[41] No more than a couple of minutes after

1730 on Friday, 7 May 1954, the Viet Minh at last reached Brigadier de Castries'
command post.

The assault team that captured it was led by Captain Ta Quang Luat. The Viet
Minh rushed into the bunker in search of de Castries, who was already standing
there waiting for them, dressed in a clean barrack-dress uniform and wearing
his scarlet Spahi cavalry side-cap. As the brigadier and his staff officers were
taken into captivity others of the communist assault team were already mounting the Viet Minh's gold-starred red flag emblazoned with the motto
'Determined to Fight and to Win' on the battered corrugated iron and sand-
bagged roof of the bunker. The communist flag was certainly flying atop the former
French command bunker at 1740. By 1820 the Viet Minh had completely occupied the former French positions that lay to the west of the Nam-Youm River and
were taking their former occupants into captivity. As night fell on 7 May, only
strong-point Isabelle still remained in French hands; although its one remaining
105mm gun had ceased firing at 1700, and at about 1900 Colonel Lalande's
troops were progressing well with the comprehensive destruction of their heavy
items of residual combat *matériel*, including the last operational M-24 tank.

Arguably, the break-out by Colonel Lalande's force from Isabelle might have
achieved a greater degree of success than in fact it did, had the high command
in Hanoi supported it more effectively. The obvious route was southwards as
Bigeard had originally envisaged. But, Lalande – by 1700 that evening well aware

Below: The last attack,
7 May 1954. Viet Minh
assault troops race
past the airstrip and
close on the centre of
the main French
Union position.

that the main position was about to fall – had had second thoughts and was contemplating moving directly towards the Viet Minh lines encircling the main position to the north, and breaking away to the cover of the western hills and valleys just short of the communist positions. He reasoned that this, being entirely unexpected, would achieve considerable surprise, and that the Viet Minh positions to the north would be largely unmanned because the troops would have moved into their newly acquired positions at Dien Bien Phu. His plan was inspired, and sufficiently audacious to have achieved some success. But his attempts to contact Hanoi by radio relay to clarify aspects of his proposal and be authorised to go ahead received no reply. So he resolved to follow the original, but predictable, plan – the southwards break-out. At 2140 the last of Isabelle's ammunition dumps and supplies began to be blown up, and at about 2200 the garrison began to move out from the positions it had occupied for some fifty-five days.

The first group acted as an advanced guard and made good progress until about 0200 on Saturday 8 May, when it was stopped by a Viet Minh force at Pom-Lot, some nine kilometres south of Isabelle. Although thirteen men managed to escape, the small force was destroyed by the communists. The second (main) group to depart Isabelle was even less lucky, being ambushed by troops of the PAVN 304th Division after having gone only one kilometre. Meanwhile, a third group (mainly Algerian troops) was engaged while it was leaving the position. To the rear of the break-out groups was a mass of walking wounded and non-combatants whose

presence in the midst of the fighting caused considerable confusion. While Colonel Lalande and others tried to regain the command bunker to make a final stand, some units and individuals, taking advantage of the confusion and the relatively limited battlefield illumination, managed to slip away into the night.[42] But the French position was clearly hopeless, and at 0150 the radio transmitter at Isabelle broadcast the fact that the sortie had failed and that there would be no further communications from Isabelle. That transmission was the very last from any part of the French Union garrison at Dien Bien Phu. It not only signalled the ultimate failure of Operation 'Castor', but heralded the imminent end of French colonial power in Indo-China, and set the scene for the eventual entry of the United States on to the Indo-Chinese battleground.

At Dien Bien Phu the guns of both sides finally fell silent, and the cease-fire was extended throughout Indo-China by General Navarre.[43]

Below: 1730 hours, Friday 7 May, 1954. Victorious Viet Minh soldiers display their flag on the top of de Castries' former command bunker.

# TRUTHS AND CONSEQUENCES
## THE BATTLE IN PERSPECTIVE

### Counting the Cost

The destruction at Dien Bien Phu of some of the best infantry and airborne units of the French army cost General Giap's divisions in the order of 23,000 casualties, many from his best-trained regular units. But France had lost 2,293 dead and 5,134 men wounded[44] since November 1953, and now most of the 11,000 men (of whom 8,158 were categorised as able-bodied or superficially wounded) who had survived and become captives on 8 May began a march to the Viet Minh prison camps, which lay many hundreds of kilometres away. For many of these exhausted (and in many cases wounded) French Union prisoners, thirty to sixty days marching twenty kilometres each day, burdened with loads of rice and the stretchers of the wounded, was beyond them. A daily ration of fourteen ounces of rice, unboiled water or (occasionally) tea, and ten peanuts every ten days, completed a process of physical breakdown which resulted in very many of these men dying en route to the camps. Of those who did survive the march, further numbers of them subsequently expired in the Viet Minh prison camps. Not surprisingly, given their prolonged period in combat, the survivors of Dien Bien Phu proved much less resilient to the privations of captivity than French prisoners who had been captured elsewhere.

Negotiations with the Viet Minh by the president of the French Red Cross at Hanoi (acting on behalf of the French high command) secured the release and evacuation of the more seriously wounded – some 1,500 in total. Inevitably, the communist victors extracted the maximum propaganda, psychological, political and military advantages from the evacuation issue, and linked the satisfying of French requests with severe constraints on French military activities elsewhere. But agreement to the removal of some 858 wounded from Dien Bien Phu was achieved on 16 May and, despite difficulties and setbacks, their evacuation had been completed by early June. Some of these wounded men were subsequently airlifted to the United States for specialist treatment.

For most of the men who had survived the march to the prison camps, where they were ill-treated, ill-fed and subjected to 'political re-education',[45] liberation and eventual repatriation came many months later, following the agreement signed at Geneva on 21 July, which ended the war and French imperial aspirations in Indo-China for ever. But of the several thousand French soldiers who had set out on the punishing march northwards after Dien Bien Phu, very many never returned home.[46] Of the sixty-one prisoners who died within three months of their release in the summer of 1954, forty-nine had been captured at Dien Bien Phu. Of the 11,000 or so French Union soldiers who were within the garrison of Dien Bien Phu when it fell on 7 and 8 May 1954, only about 3,000 – including the 858 wounded men and twenty-seven medical staff who had been repatriated under the terms of the 16 May agreement – ever returned to France.

Despite the ultimate futility of the defence of Dien Bien Phu, it had neverthe-less demonstrated the courage, tenacious fighting ability and dedication of these regular French soldiers and their North African comrades. Many later observed that these gallant men had merited neither the inadequate political leadership in Paris nor the less than professional military leadership in Hanoi and Saigon that had sent them to Dien Bien Phu.

In accordance with the terms of the Geneva Agreement, the last French Union troops in Indo-China finally departed Hanoi on 9 October 1954.

Opposite page: The steadily rising numbers of French casualties placed an ever-increasing medical and logistic burden upon the garrison.

## End of an Empire

In France the political consequences of the war were traumatic, and Laniel's administration did not long survive. The discrediting of Laniel was exemplified by the hostile reception that he and President René Coty received from the people of Paris during their attendance at the annual VE-Day celebrations at the Arc de Triomphe on Saturday 8 May, just twenty-four hours after the fall of the main position at Dien Bien Phu. Significantly, one Brigadier General Charles de Gaulle, who was attending the event in no official capacity, received a very different reception from the assembled crowds that day; a man whose climb to political power was much accelerated in the wake of France's loss of Indo-China. In 1958 the French Fourth Republic also fell, though Indo-China was but one of several contributory issues and failures that brought this about.

But while governments may come and go, and defeated or discredited politi-cians regularly re-invent themselves to fight (metaphorically) another day, this option was not available to the almost 82,000 French, French Foreign Legion, North and West African and Vietnamese national army soldiers who had died during nine years of fighting in Indo-China. Although the communists emerged as the victors, they too had paid a very heavy price for their success; some estimates of their dead being put as high as 150,000 over the same period. Nevertheless, Ho and Giap could still be well pleased. Laos, Cambodia and North and South Vietnam were now independent states, the boundary between communist North Vietnam and the non-communist Republic of South Vietnam having been set by the Geneva conference at the 17th Parallel. Apart from the fact that part of Vietnam was still under non-communist control, the two leaders and their supporters in Beijing and Moscow could reflect with considerable satisfaction on the campaign that the Viet Minh had conducted since the defeat of the Japanese in 1945.

## The Political and Strategic Perspectives

Why then was the French defeat in Indo-China so comprehensive and – for many French political and military leaders – so unexpected? The reasons for the catastrophe of 1954 were both political and military. At the outset, the French government of 1945 had faced the formidable task of healing a divided nation following the Vichy years, and endeavouring to restore the former power and glory of France. Part of this process involved the re-acquisition and retention of the pre-1940 French colonial empire. But France was no longer a great power, and its leaders seriously misjudged the mood of the post-war world – that of the United States in particular – with regard to European imperialism and colonialism. Many Americans would argue that these 'isms' of the pre-1939 world had already drawn the United States into two world wars. If, in 1945, France had declared an intention simply to stabilise its possessions in Indo-China, prior to granting them full independence, Paris might have undercut the communist and nationalist coalition and weakened the nationalist cause, perhaps even attracting the latter's active support. Such a policy might also have been looked upon favourably by the United States if and when France requested American support to achieve it.

In post-invasion, post-Vichy, post-occupation and post-war France, however, popular attitudes were such that nothing short of a return to the pre-1940 *status quo* was acceptable. So the government of the Fourth Republic was determined to restore French dominance in Indo-China, rather than follow the traditional republican ideals of *liberté*, *égalité* and *fraternité*. It followed that the so-called independence talks conducted from 1947 to 1950, based upon the return of the Emperor Bao Dai as a puppet ruler, were no more than a rather transparent device to maintain French dominance of the region.

The adoption of a more enlightened French policy for Indo-China might well have produced a satisfactory settlement before 1953; thereby pre-empting the significant support provided to the Viet Minh by China after the armistice in Korea. In such circumstances, it is also less likely that the Soviets would have chosen to embrace Ho Chi Minh's cause so wholeheartedly, especially if the war had ended before the Soviet Union's successful atom bomb test on 23 September 1949, when Stalin's attention was also focused primarily upon Europe.

But after the Cao Bang disaster, the French people viewed the war in Indo-China with an ambivalence that combined concern with something amounting to denial. While there were increasingly strident protests and calls from the left for an end to the war and for France to grant Indo-China its independence, there was never a readily identifiable mass protest movement against the war. Part of the reason for this was that much of the war was being fought for France by foreigners. These included the French Foreign Legion, units of the Armeé d'Afrique (principally the Algerians and Moroccans) and the pro-French Vietnamese national army, plus various other Indo-Chinese military units and indigenous tribes. Also, only regular French soldiers and volunteers were permitted to serve in Indo-China.

The French Assembly's conscription decision denied the high command in Indo-China the manpower it needed to conduct a successful counter-revolutionary campaign. As a result, the French commanders in Indo-China received only a fraction of the men and *matériel* that they required to accomplish their mission; and this was a deciding factor in what was to become a war of attrition. Giap fully appreciated that this was so when he stated in late 1950 that 'The enemy will pass slowly from the offensive to the defensive. The *Blitzkrieg* will transform itself into a war of long duration. Thus, the enemy will be caught in a dilemma: he has to drag out the war in order to win it and does not possess, on the other hand, the psychological and political means to fight a long-drawn-out war.'[47] Giap's words later proved just as prophetic during the next conflict in South-East Asia.

Had the French catastrophe at Cao Bang not occurred, with the consequent block on ordinary French conscripts serving in Indo-China, the views and reactions of the French public to the war might have been very different. But, given a conflict that was taking place far away, being fought exclusively by professional soldiers and foreigners, the French people allowed themselves the luxury of hoping for a victory and the restoration of French glory, while simultaneously distancing themselves from the actualities of the war; and in some cases even indicating an abhorrence of it and those who fought it on their behalf. This last was exemplified by the fact that those casualties arriving in Paris from Indo-China could not be conveyed openly across Paris because of the administration's fear of possible left-wing demonstrations. In similar vein, it had been decided that, if necessary, blood donors in France would be advised that their blood would not be used for the casualties of Indo-China.[48]

Even if the high command had received the necessary resources, however, the conduct of the French military campaign still left a great deal to be desired. The history of France and her empire is littered with the divergence between the valiant efforts of her soldiers and the professional shortcomings of those who commanded them at the highest level. In Indo-China much of the potentially formidable French combat potential was once again often misdirected or squandered by political and military ineptitude at the highest levels.

From the very beginning of the war in 1946, the French made the fundamental error of assessing incorrectly the nature and capability of the Viet Minh. Consequently, they applied traditional concepts of conventional warfare – where the destruction of the enemy was the overriding priority – to deal with the much more complex nature of a revolutionary war. This initial misconception was symptomatic of the overall failure of French strategic intelligence in South-East Asia throughout the war.

Starting from such a major error, it is perhaps no surprise that there was such a lack of intelligence, or of the correct interpretation of the intelligence that was available, prior to and during the battle of Dien Bien Phu.[49] The failure of the artillery assessment is a striking example of this, it having been a major contributor to the French defeat. At the same time, the correlation between events on the battlefield and the political and information management perspectives were not understood. Therefore, the French military campaign was conducted more or less in isolation from these complementary activities. It followed that the French never really addressed, and so could not reasonably have hoped to win, the 'hearts and minds' campaign in Indo-China. For their part, Ho Chi Minh and

Giap understood very well the vital importance of these adjuncts to the military campaign.

Throughout the war, the communists sought and generally gained (either by reward or coercion) the support of the people of northern Indo-China. They were therefore able to live and operate within the civilian community, whereas the French were constrained to operate from their bases, and so were never able to reverse the support of the people for the Viet Minh. If de Tassigny had been given the resources to do so, he might have been able to adopt a similar scheme of 'new villages' to that which Briggs and Templer were employing in Malaya at about the same time. But in Malaya the aim of this concept was to remove and so deny support to the Chinese minority terrorists, whereas the French approach was to create locations at or from which the Viet Minh could be destroyed, so it would be wrong to infer close parallels between the new villages of Malaya and the new forts of Indo-China. The latter, with the implied expectation of combat, also required considerable quantities of manpower both at the forts and to reinforce them if under attack. It was therefore an inappropriate strategy for a force that always suffered from severe manpower constraints throughout the war. Moreover, when reaction forces or reinforcements were sent to assist a beleaguered fort, they usually moved either by vehicle on the relatively few roads or (when boats or amphibious vehicles were available) by river, thereby falling prey to Viet Minh ambushes.

Finally, the French relied heavily upon the ready availability of their national air-power to support the ground forces. Their several successes against the Viet Minh in 1951 and at the end of 1952 supported the view that this was the panacea that would win the war. Nowhere was the fallacy of this more evident than at Dien Bien Phu, by which time Giap had correctly assessed the danger posed to his forces from the air, and had developed the necessary anti-aircraft defence to counter this threat.[50]

### The Operational and Tactical Perspectives

Most of the reasons for the final defeat of the French Union forces in their several strong-points at Dien Bien Phu, straddling the Nam-Youm River, between November 1953 and May 1954, have already emerged from the foregoing text. But it is only when these reasons are viewed together that the true scale of the errors and miscalculations involved becomes clear.

It would be a mistake, however, to lay the blame for the defeat at Dien Bien Phu almost exclusively on French errors and weaknesses. To do so would be unfair to the capability of the Viet Minh under their long-standing commander General Vo Nguyen Giap. After all, it was Giap's correct appreciation of French strengths and weaknesses that permitted him to counter or exploit them to produce the communist victory despite the French technology. In fact, unlike many great battles, where the intellectual struggle between the opposing commanders is every bit as significant as the combat power, deployment and capabilities of their forces on the ground, in the case of Dien Bien Phu it was really only Giap who stood out as the great operational commander.

Unquestionably the tactical command skills and leadership of Langlais, Bigeard and Lalande on the battlefield were consistently outstanding, and in several cases frustrated and delayed the achievement of Giap's tactical aspirations at Dien Bien Phu; but the battle could never be characterised as a struggle between two great military minds, given the absence of any such identifiable commander on the French side. Patently, the strategic and operational command of Dien Bien Phu was at best an amalgam of the actions and input of de Castries, Cogny and Navarre on the French side, the divergences between whom were always central to the flawed nature of Operations 'Castor' and 'Pollux'. Certainly

Below: Once air evacuation ceased, the conditions for the French Union wounded deteriorated rapidly, notwithstanding the best efforts of the medical personnel.

the difficult personal relationship and ambivalence of General Navarre and Major General Cogny concerning their perceptions of the role of Dien Bien Phu greatly assisted Giap by weakening the planning concepts that underwrote the French Union garrison's existence. But here again Giap knew his enemy very well and was able to profit from these flaws and problems in the French high command and exploit them to such decisive effect.

But above all else, Giap's understanding of the need to concentrate the Viet Minh forces in overwhelming strength, and at the same time force or delude the French into dissipating the strength of their own forces, was fundamental to the achievement of his success. Only by applying his greatest asset – manpower – in irresistible numbers at Dien Bien Phu could he hope to counter the (albeit overstated) technology, air- and fire-power of the French Union forces. Admittedly, Giap's initial adherence to the tactical advice of his Chinese advisers probably resulted in greater numbers of Viet Minh casualties than might have been strictly necessary. But whenever the communists sustained their highest losses, this was often attributable to Giap (who was constantly under time constraints because of the approaching monsoon and the political need of a victory) having underestimated the resilience of a dwindling French Union garrison that was bolstered time and again by the personal leadership of certain of its key tactical commanders: notably Langlais, Bigeard and Lalande. But even here, Giap might be forgiven for underestimating the determination of those French Union soldiers whose situation most military pundits would have thought hopeless at a very early stage in the battle – certainly after the failure of Operation 'Pollux'.

The relative strengths assessments carried out by the high commands of each side were central to the outcome of the battle. It was ever thus in military conflicts, and the failures of French intelligence – but more importantly the failure of the French high command to heed much of that which the intelligence staff produced – has already been highlighted; together with the equally dangerous over-estimation of the capabilities of the French Union forces vis-à-vis those of the Viet Minh. Although Giap on at least two occasions decided prematurely that Dien Bien Phu was ready to fall, and launched major assaults that failed to achieve this, overall his analysis and deductions were entirely accurate. Foremost among these were his awareness that the Viet Minh had to defeat or otherwise neutralise French fire- and air-power at Dien Bien Phu, and linked to the latter was the need to win the logistics battle which would in turn permit the communists to win the war.

**Air-Power**

At Dien Bien Phu the Viet Minh shot down forty-eight French aircraft, damaged 167 in the air and destroyed fourteen on the ground. With a standard planning allocation of 100 transport or supply aircraft and seventy-five combat aircraft to support Dien Bien Phu, these losses were a severe drain on the French air force mission to support operations throughout French Indo-China. The number and effectiveness of the Viet Minh anti-aircraft guns (and the support for them provided by the communist Chinese soldiers) was a key factor in Giap's victory; for it neutralised the ability of the French to write down the Viet Minh artillery and imposed a stranglehold on the garrison's only viable means of supply and reinforcement, while at the same time reducing the French air force's ability to interdict the communist lines of communication.

The effect of the Viet Minh anti-aircraft plan on the garrison at Dien Bien Phu was akin to the precarious situation of a mediaeval castle entirely surrounded by a besieging force, with water the only natural resource available within the castle walls. Had the French possessed air assets in vastly greater numbers they might have been able to support the garrison effectively over a limited period, and so enable its relief or withdrawal – via Operations 'Condor' or 'Albatros'. But at the end of the Second World War the size and capability of the French air force was entirely inadequate for this and so the point is academic. Similarly, had the United States and other nations been minded to carry out Operation 'Vulture', or to commit their air-power wholeheartedly to the general air campaign in support of the French, the Viet Minh position at Dien Bien Phu might well have become untenable and the garrison might have been saved; although even in these circumstances it would not have been able to fulfil its role as envisaged by either Navarre or Cogny. And in any case, the final outcome of the war would have been merely delayed, rather than significantly different. But the international implications of such a widening of the war would certainly have been dire (including the possible use of atomic weapons), and it was probably unrealistic of the French government to have sought or expected overt international military support in the first place. Nevertheless, the lack of US support at this desperate time was another factor affecting France's future relations with Washington and contributed to increasing French disaffection with aspects of the command and control arrangements of NATO. This in due course fed the rising tide of French nationalism post-Indo-China and the increasing political prominence of General Charles de Gaulle.

**Logistics**

Closely linked to the air campaign was the whole business of logistics, reinforcement and re-supply. In simple terms, notwithstanding a moderately effective (but never in great enough numbers) French air force interdiction campaign against the Viet Minh lines of communication from the Chinese border down to and along Route 41, the Viet Minh were always able to generate quantities of manpower and *matériel* sufficient not only to sustain and reinforce their existing forces (some five divisions, with a total strength that well exceeded 40,000 men throughout all but the first few weeks of the battle), but also progressively to increase their real combat capability. They did this by the addition of new weapon systems, such as additional anti-aircraft guns and the Katyusha multiple

rocket-launchers, by building up reserves held close to the valley in concentration areas, and by stockpiling sufficient ammunition to ensure that there would
be no loss of momentum when the final attack was launched.

This situation contrasted starkly with that of the French, whose manpower
and *matériel* resources were inadequate for the task almost from the beginning
of Operation 'Castor', and then dwindled as the conflict progressed. Quite apart

from the inappropriate choice of Dien Bien Phu for the role that it subsequently assumed, the number of French Union combat units (in reality, there were at most only the equivalent of ten infantry battalions ever in place at Dien Bien Phu at any specific moment) was insufficient to counter the overwhelming numbers of Viet Minh infantrymen that Giap launched against them. The failure of the French Union artillery both to counter that of the Viet Minh, and then to replace its losses to communist fire, together with the directly related and absolutely critical paucity of engineer stores and construction equipment provided to Dien Bien Phu, sealed the fate of the garrison even before the key battles from mid-March had begun. Once battle was joined, and as more and more communist troops and *matériel* flowed into the Dien Bien Phu valley, the French Union forces fell ever farther behind in the race to generate essential resources and win the vital logistics battle.

**The Human Element**

Despite the crucial importance of *matériel* and other equipment and weapons considerations, in the final analysis, the battle of Dien Bien Phu, as in any other armed conflict, was won by human beings – soldiers – and by those who led them on the battlefield. Self-evidently, the nature of the Viet Minh soldier was fundamentally different from that of the French Union force (the soldiers of the French Vietnamese units excepted). Similarly, the unit organisation and equipment of the Viet Minh units was altogether different from that of the French. But the main difference between the Viet Minh and the French Union forces was motivation. The bravery, discipline, robustness and determination of the Viet Minh were remarkable throughout the battle, particularly in light of their losses; only during the desperate fighting of mid-April were there clear signs of disquiet in some Viet Minh units. But whereas the communist soldiers were fighting for a cause and for Vietnamese independence, the French Union forces – very many of whom were North African and other colonial troops, Vietnamese, T'ai and legionnaires – were fighting to maintain a French colonial empire: a somewhat incongruous cause given the national and ethnic composition of the garrison. The fact that by the end of the battle there were about 4,000 internal deserters – the Rats of the Nam-Youm – within the garrison was stark testimony to the poor motivation and morale of many French Union individuals and units whose contribution to the

Left: Aftermath of battle. Columns of defeated French Union soldiers are marched away from Dien Bien Phu, closely guarded by their Viet Minh captors. Very many of these men were not to survive their time in communist captivity.

battle was sorely missed and rightly resented by those who continued to man the trenches and bunkers of Dien Bien Phu. Consequently, those who fought best – generally the paratroops of all nationalities and the legionnaires, plus some other groups – fought, as ever, primarily for their leaders (such as Langlais, Bigeard and Lalande, and many other battalion, company and platoon commanders), for their comrades and for the honour of their regiments rather than for any higher French political or ideological cause, and from this they drew the remarkable strength that time and again enabled them against all odds to halt or throw back the communist assaults.

Indeed, the ordinary French Union soldiers, including their comrades of the Vietnamese national army, the Foreign Legion and the Armée d'Afrique, deserved a better cause to fight for in Indo-China, and better leadership at the highest political and military levels; and the almost six months of fighting at Dien Bien Phu exemplified this. Their overall conduct during the eight-year Indo-China conflict was remarkable, and their fighting abilities at unit level were almost without exception in the best traditions of the great days of the old French army. So although the war in Indo-China was an inglorious period in terms of French political and international history, for many of the regiments that fought there it provided an opportunity to build upon their already proud history and record of selfless dedication to the needs and policies of France. But in Indo-China many of these men found that their destiny was being determined by a government and political agenda that did not measure up to the standards of honour, duty and discipline of an army that was becoming increasingly de-coupled from Paris – both geographically and philosophically; and just seven years later, in Algeria in 1961, a revolt by some of the most illustrious units of the French army demonstrated the true extent of this deteriorating situation. Numerous members of the Algerian nationalist FLN and ALN forces that these French airborne and Foreign Legion units fought during the Algerian war of independence had previously served as members of the French Union forces; for many, the seeds of that war in North Africa were sown during their time in Indo-China, and for some this was undoubtedly as a result of their experiences during the battle at Dien Bien Phu and while in communist captivity following the French Union defeat.

### The Seeds of Future Conflict

By the close of 1954 the French struggle in Vietnam, Laos and Cambodia was at an end, while at Geneva the foundations for what is often termed the 'Second Indo-China War' – the American Vietnam War – were already being laid.[51] And for President Ho Chi Minh and General Vo Nguyen Giap this new conflict was merely the next phase of their great mission to impose their form of nationalism and communist rule upon the whole of a unified Vietnam: a long campaigning road, on which the most significant milestone of all had without a doubt been the battle of Dien Bien Phu.

# BIBLIOGRAPHY

Allaire, Lt. Jacques. 'Le 6e BPC à Dien Bien Phu' in *La Charte* (Mars-Avril), Paris, 2003

Bergot, Erwan. *1954: 'Eliane' – La Bataille des Paras*. Histoire et Collections, Paris, 1987

Boury, M. Paul. 'La Bataille d'Hoa Binh: Une Page de Gloire dans la Guerre d'Indochine' in *Képi Blanc* (Mai), Aubagne, 2002

Cadiou, Yves L. and Szecsko, Tibor. *French Foreign Legion: 1940 to the Present*. Arms & Armour Press, London, 1986

Delperier, Louis. *La Guerre d'Indochine*. Histoire et Collections, Paris, 1988

Fall, Bernard B. *Street Without Joy: Insurgency in Indo-China, 1946–63*. Pall Mall Press, London and Dunmow, 1963

— *Hell in a Very Small Place – The Siege of Dien Bien Phu*. Pall Mall Press, London and Oxford, 1967

Fischer, Guillaume. *Les Camps*. Histoire et Collections, Paris, 1989

Foss, Christopher F. *Armoured Fighting Vehicles of the World*. Ian Allan Ltd., London, 1971

Fowler, Will, ed. Philip de Sainte-Croix. *Airborne Operations in French Indo-China*. Salamander Books Ltd., London, 1978

Freedman, Lawrence. *The Cold War*. Cassell, London, 2001

Geraghty, Tony. *March or Die*. Grafton Books, London, 1986

Hammond, Dr. William Michael, ed. Ray Bonds. *The Vietnam War*. Salamander Books Ltd., London, 1979

Hel, Christian. *Le Dernier Combat sur Isabelle 7 et 8 Mai 1954*. Histoire et Collections, Paris, 1989

Isaacs, Jeremy and Downey, Taylor. *Cold War*. Bantam Press, London, 1998

Isby, David C. *Weapons and Tactics of the Soviet Army*. Jane's Publ. Co. Ltd., London, 1981

Lartéguy, Jean. *The Lost Command*. Arrow Books Ltd, London, 1966 (fact-based fiction)

Lassus, Dennis. *6 Mois de Combat à Dien Bien Phu*. Histoire et Collections, Paris, 1989

Loiseau, Dr. Y. 'Les Mortiers Lourds des Unités Parachutistes de la Légion Étrangère' in *Képi Blanc* (Juin), Aubagne, 2002

Macdonald, Peter. *Giap: The Victor in Vietnam*. Fourth Estate Ltd, London, 1993

McCuen, John J. *The Art of Counter-Revolutionary War*. Faber and Faber, London, 1966

Mercer, Charles. *The Foreign Legion*. Four Square Books, London, 1964

Mesko, Jim. *Armor in Vietnam*. Squadron/Signal Publications Inc., Carrollton, Texas, 1982

Newman, Bernard. *Background to Viet-Nam*. Robert Hale, London, 1965

Philip, Craig. *Last Stands: Famous Battles Against the Odds*. Grange Books plc, London, 1994

Pimlott, John. *War in Peace: Ho Chi Minh's Triumph*. Orbis Publ., London, 1981

Randa, Philippe. *Bigeard Attaque à Diên Biên Phu*. Histoire et Collections, Paris, 1989

Roy, Jules. *The Battle of Dien Bien Phu*. Harper & Row, New York, Faber and Faber, London, 1965

Sicard, Jacques. *Les Formations Paras en Indochine*. Histoire et Collections, Paris, 1988

Stone, David. *Wars of the Cold War: Campaigns and Conflicts 1945–1990*. Brassey's, London, 2004

— 'The Supreme Adventure: The Life and Death of Lieutenant Colonel Pierre Jeanpierre of the French Foreign Legion' in *British Army Review*, No. 98, August, 1991

Szecsko, Tibor. *Le Grand Livre des Insignes de la Légion Étrangère*. IILE/SIHLE, Le Coteau, 1991

Thompson, Sir Robert. *War in Peace: Vietnam*. Orbis Publ., London, 1981

Von Senger und Etterlin, Dr. F. M. *The World's Armoured Fighting Vehicles*. Macdonald, London, 1962

Watson, Dr. George M. and O'Neill, Richard. *The Vietnam War: The End of French Rule in Indo-China*. Salamander Books, London, 1979

Wiener, Friedrich. *The Armies of the Warsaw Pact*. Carl Uberreuter Publ., Vienna, 1978

Windrow, Martin. *French Foreign Legion*. Osprey, 1971

— *Uniforms of the French Foreign Legion 1831–1981*. Blandford Press, Poole, Dorset, 1986

— *The French Indo-China War 1945-54*. Osprey, 1998

Windrow, Martin and Brady, Wayne. *French Foreign Legion Paratroops*. Osprey, 1985

Young, John Robert. *The French Foreign Legion*. Thames and Hudson, London, 1985

Young, Marilyn B. *The Vietnam Wars 1945–1990*. Harper Collins Publ./Harper Perennial, New York, 1991

# NOTES

**Author's Note**

1 These include Bernard Fall's *Hell in a Very Small Place* and Jules Roy's *Battle of Dien Bien Phu*.

**Preface**

2 But the French government misused much of its allocated Marshall Aid to fund its colonial wars, instead of regenerating and stabilising post-1945 France.

3 Pragmatically, France has consistently ensured that its armed forces are not subject to the invasive legislation on Human Rights that has adversely affected the overall quality of several other Western armies since the mid-1990s. Far from feeling disadvantaged, many members of the French regular army derive considerable pride from this arrangement, which sets them apart from and above what they regard as a materialistic, excessively litigious, and 'soft' modern French civilian society (views expressed to the author by French officers and soldiers in the former Yugoslavia, 1995 and 1996).

**Chapter 1**

4 Vo Nguyen Giap was born on 28 August 1911 in An-Xa, a village near the 17th Parallel. Giap had two sisters and was the elder of two sons. The family was one of poor farmers, although Giap's father was educated and a scholar by local standards; he was also a committed nationalist, and in 1919 he was arrested for subversion, dying in prison a few weeks later. Giap's sister was arrested shortly after this and, although not detained long, became ill in prison. She died soon after her release. Meanwhile, Giap showed academic aptitude, and attended the Lycée Nationale in Hue from 1924. Although strongly anti-colonialism, he was fluent in French and admired French culture and learning. From 1924 to 1925 Giap became increasingly politically active, which resulted in his name appearing on French security service files. In 1926 he was expelled for anti-colonial activities and returned An Xa, where he joined the Tan Viet Cach Meng Dang nationalist underground movement. Subsequently he converted to communism. Later, he returned to Hue, where he was again involved in political protest movements. Inevitably, arrest followed, but he was released after serving three months of a two years' sentence. Still a high academic achiever, he studied philosophy, and graduated in July 1937 as a lawyer with degrees in law and political economics. That same year he joined the Indo-Chinese Communist Party (ICP). In June 1938 he married Nguyen Thi Minh Giang, who was also a committed nationalist and communist. Together they rose within the organisation and were soon numbered among the top ten leaders of the ICP. Giap wrote extensively in support of his political activities, but this impacted adversely upon his studies and he failed to qualify for a Certificate of Administrative Law, which prevented him from practising. Consequently, he took up the teaching of history at the Thang Long Private School in Hanoi. In May 1939 his daughter Hong An was born. Meanwhile, his sister-in-law, who had studied communism in Russia during the late 1930s, had returned to Saigon – where she was arrested, imprisoned, and subsequently executed. This was the third personal tragedy for Giap. In 1939 the Communist Party was banned and on 3 May 1940 Giap fled to China. His wife returned home to Vinh, but there she was arrested, tried, and sentenced to fifteen years in Hoa Lo Central Prison, Hanoi. In June 1940 Giap at last met Ho Chi Minh. Their initial plans to train and work for the movement in China changed shortly afterwards, following the German defeat of France, and their focus reverted to Indo-China where the Vichy authorities and the Japanese (in the north) were administering the country. Giap's practical and military action perfectly balanced Ho's philosophical approach to their political goals. Then, in mid-1943, Giap's wife died in prison: a fourth personal tragedy that Giap could attribute directly to the French colonial authorities, one that affected and hardened him significantly.

5 In December 1949, at the end of the Chinese Civil War, the victorious Mao Tse-tung recognised the Democratic Republic of Vietnam and implemented a programme to provide advice, *matériel* and training to the Viet Minh. In October 1951 a rail link into China was completed, the Chinese arsenal at Kunming was exclusively assigned to support the Viet Minh, and in 1951 China gave the Viet Minh 4,000 tons of weapons and munitions (including 75mm cannon, Skoda rifles, German artillery guns, 100,000 grenades, 10,000 rounds of 75mm ammunition and ten million rounds of rifle ammunition. In 1952 China provided a further 40,000 rifles, 4,000 machine-guns, a number of 120mm recoilless rifles, thirty-five field guns, and fifty light anti-aircraft guns. Finally, by December 1952, 40,000 Viet Minh soldiers and 10,000 officers had been trained in Chinese military schools.

6 Previously, in March 1948, the Viet Minh had divided the country into six operational zones: the Red River delta, north-west Tonkin, north-east Tonkin, north Annam, south Annam, and Cochin China. By the end of 1948 Ho and Giap had already assessed that the greater proportion of the population was committed to the liberation of Vietnam from French rule.

7 In April 1949 there were thirty-two regular battalions and 137 regional battalions. In May 1950 Ho directed that all males in Annam and Tonkin aged sixteen to fifty-five were required to serve with the Viet Minh, and by June 1951 there were 117 regular battalions (all organised into regiments) and thirty-seven regional battalions. These regular regiments in turn formed divisions of about 10,000 men each. These included the 304th, 308th (Iron Division), 312th, 316th and 320th (Mekong Delta). In addition, by mid-1952 the 351st Heavy Division (comprised primarily of artillery and engineer units) was also operational.

Each division was supported by 50,000 porters who were required to carry 55 pounds of rice or 40 pounds of other stores 25 kilometres by day, 20 kilometres at night, or half as much half as far over mountainous terrain. The Viet Minh logistics system also used buffalo carts carrying 770 pounds twelve kilometres per day and horse carts carrying 470 pounds 20 kilometres per day.

8 Eight years later, as a lieutenant colonel, Jeanpierre commanded 1 REP (1er Régiment Étranger de Parachutistes) in Algeria, where he was killed in action while leading his legionnaires against ALN guerrillas on 29 May 1958. See David Stone's *The Supreme Adventure: The Life and Death of Lieutenant Colonel Pierre Jeanpierre of the French Foreign Legion*.

9 General Jean de Lattre de Tassigny fell seriously ill with cancer during 1951 and soon had to return to France. He died in Paris in January 1952. His premature departure from Indo-China denied the French Union forces a commander who might well have been able to conduct an effective and balanced overall strategy against General Giap and the Viet Minh; but the eventual departure of the French from Indo-China would still probably only have been delayed rather than avoided.

10 The base at Na San was subsequently evacuated without any loss of French lives during a rationalisation and reduction of the number of French outstations in August 1953.

## Chapter 2

11 Many in the French high command underestimated the uniquely tribal nature of the T'ai, Meo and other Montagnard tribesmen who fought with and for them. These tribesmen were fiercely independent of any central Vietnamese government control and were content to fight for the French wherever they identified that to do so was in their tribal interests. Although in many respects similar, the Meo and T'ai groups spoke different languages and would certainly have regarded one another as foreigners. Consequently, where these tribes were employed to fight in their own territory, they were a very effective asset; but once removed from their land and families to match the needs of a wider military strategy their effectiveness in combat declined markedly.

12 Some accounts of Dien Bien Phu published in the 1960s indicate an even greater disparity between the height of the hills within the valley and those surrounding it. The figures adopted in this account are based on a 1989 analysis that utilised modern cartographic techniques, but this more recent analysis does not detract to any extent from the overall conclusion in earlier accounts that all positions in the valley could be dominated by view and by fire from the high ground that surrounded it.

## Chapter 3

13 The GCMA units were re-designated Groupements Mixtes d'Intervention (GMI) in December 1953.

## Chapter 4

14 See *Képi Blanc* No. 634, June 2002, p. 50.

15 Christian Marie Ferdinand de la Criox de Castries was born in Paris on 11 August 1902. Determined on a military career, he enlisted as a private soldier, and was eventually commissioned. Highlights of his service as a cavalry officer during the Second World War included a courageous three-day stand against superior German air and ground forces in 1940, escape from a prisoner of war camp following his capture in 1941, and – from mid-1944 – distinguished service with the French 1st Army in mainland Europe. Post-war, he commanded a *Groupement Mobile* (GM) in the Red River delta area of Indo-China. Nevertheless, neither de Castries' personality and armoured cavalry background nor the specific nature of his previous military experience in Indo-China particularly well suited him for command of the defensive operation at Dien Bien Phu.

16 Command of the several strong-points and subordinate positions changed as commanders became casualties, as the operational situation changed, and as the deployment and command and control of the garrison units was modified. Although ostensibly but a part of the Dien Bien Phu defensive position, Isabelle soon became cut off and isolated from the main position. Throughout the battle Isabelle was commanded by Lieutenant Colonel André Lalande (who was promoted colonel on 16 April 1954).

## Chapter 6

17 Insights into Giap's thinking, assessments and planning for Dien Bien Phu can be found in Peter Macdonald's *Giap The Victor*. In 1990 Macdonald was invited to visit Hanoi for the express purpose of interviewing Giap, and his work provides a useful and often unique perspective on Giap himself, as well as a full account of his wars in Vietnam against both the French and the Americans.

18 Fall's *Hell in a Very Small Place*. p. 377 refers to 'Soviet-made *Katyusha* 6-tube field rockets' and '… between twelve to sixteen of the 6-tube *Katyusha* rocket-launchers', p. 451, but the author has been unable to trace the origin of this description, as apparently no 6-tube MRL system was then available (either in service or obsolete) from Soviet or PLA sources. Another explanation (though without supporting evidence) could be that BM-13 tubes might have been dismounted and used individually or in groups of six tubes. Certainly, during the later war against the United States in Vietnam the Viet Cong used dismounted BM-21 MRL tubes in this way, see Isby, *Weapons and Tactics of the Soviet Army*, p. 203.

## Chapter 7

19 Pierre Charles Albert Marie Langlais was born at Pontivy in Morbihan, Brittany on 2 December 1909. He had chosen a military career and sought advancement via service in the ranks. However, he passed the entrance examination for St-Cyr and gained his commission. Thereafter, he opted for Saharan service – where he felt that the constant armed clashes and hard living would broaden his professional experience. The harsh desert environment well-suited a man described as isolated, hard and self-sufficient. During the Second World War he served with French forces in Italy, France and Germany. Post-war he first went to Indo-China in

October 1945, with the 9th Colonial Infantry Division, and participated in the early reoccupation battles of 1946 and that for Hanoi in the spring of 1947. During his second Indo-China tour, in 1949, he served on the Chinese border. Later he served in northern Laos and central Vietnam. He then returned to France and qualified as a paratrooper in order to follow Brigadier General Jean Gilles as commander of the 1st Colonial Half Brigade of Paratroop Commandos. As a lieutenant colonel, he returned to Indo-China for his third two-year tour there, as commander of GAP 2: the appointment that took him to Dien Bien Phu in 1953. He was promoted colonel during the battle. Captured at the end of the battle in May 1954, he was subsequently repatriated, remained in the army and rose further in rank. However, once retired, in ill health, he did not prosper as had his colleague Bigeard. In 1988, he fell to his death from a window in a high-rise building.

20 5 BPVN had subsequently been withdrawn from Dien Bien Phu on 25 January, when air-landed infantry units relieved some of the original parachute battalions.

21 Langlais took immediate and drastic disciplinary action against those officers and Vietnamese soldiers of 5 BPVN that had refused to advance. He dismissed them from the unit and sent them to exist unsupported as non-accredited local labourers within the base area.

22 An initial attempt to cover up the true circumstances of Piroth's death within the garrison and in Hanoi meant that his suicide may have taken place as late as the night of 18/19 March or (Roy, pp. 174–5) as early as the night of 14/15 March, although most French and English accounts have settled the date as being on the night or early morning of 15/16 March.

23 It is unclear as to what extent de Castries had known Keller previously or had influenced his appointment as chief of staff, although that of Piroth as artillery commander was almost certainly made arbitrarily by Major General Cogny (also a former artillery officer) in Hanoi with little, if any, consultation with de Castries.

24 6 BPC had been withdrawn from Dien Bien Phu on 11 December, when air-landed infantry units relieved some of the original parachute battalions.

25 Marcel Maurice 'Bruno' Bigeard was born on 14 February 1916, the son of a railway worker. In 1936 he was called for national service and served with the 23e Régiment d'Infanterie de Forteresse in the forward defences of the Maginot Line at Haguenau. In civilian life, he was employed as a bank clerk in a branch of Société Générale at Toul. At the outbreak of the Second World War he was recalled to duty and served in the 79e Régiment d'Infanterie de Forteresse, achieving NCO's rank. He was soon disillusioned by the inertia and defeatist attitudes he encountered in the French army of 1939. By 1941 he was a sergeant and had already won several awards for bravery, but that year he was captured by the Germans. After two unsuccessful attempts, he escaped from his prison camp and joined a French colonial unit in North Africa as sous-lieutenant. Subsequently, he was trained as a paratrooper by the British, and in 1944 – with the nomi-

nal rank of 'major' – he was dropped into the département of Ariège to fight with the Maquis; he took part in the liberation of Foix on 19 August and was awarded the British DSO. After the war he served with the 23e Régiment d'Infanterie Coloniale. He was now a captain and had married. His first tour of duty in Indo-China, for which he volunteered in order to broaden his military experience, was in 1945. By 1948 he was a company commander in a T'ai Vietnamese battalion. On 12 November 1950 he left Indo-China for a tour of duty in France, but in July 1952 he returned (as a major) to assume command of the élite 6e Bataillon de Parachutistes Coloniaux (6 BPC), then 1,000 strong. During the months that followed 6 BPC was constantly engaged in combat, notably at Tu-Le, Na San and Lang-Son, as well as in numerous commando-type operations in the Red River delta and elsewhere in Tonkin. In November 1953 he was still the commanding officer of 6 BPC. At Dien Bien Phu he was promoted lieutenant colonel. He was captured on 7 May 1954. Repatriated, he remained in the army and achieved the rank of general, and became a Deputy in the National Assembly. He retired at the end of his service as one of France's most decorated (including twenty-five awards for valour), best-known and respected soldiers of the twentieth century. He retired to Toul and in 1975 wrote the first of several books and also involved himself in French politics. At the age of 75 Bigeard was still jogging (usually beside the river Moselle) seven kilometres each morning and five in the evening, and routinely swimming ten lengths of the pool. He is still alive, and still lives in Toul.

## Chapter 8

26 While the precise circumstances are unclear, it appears that the staff in Hanoi had been dilatory in processing de Castries' urgent request for an additional airborne battalion, made on the evening of 30 March, and that because of a social engagement that evening Cogny was not updated on the evolving situation before 0745 the next day, when (somewhat embarrassingly for Cogny) General Navarre was visiting him. Nevertheless, there was still time to act, but the commanders and their staff then invoked the policy of not conducting parachute drops by day because of the risks involved. Consequently, the troops needed to reinforce and replace the soldiers of 6 BPC, 8 BPC and 5 BPVN on recaptured Dominique and Eliane remained at their airfield at Hanoi throughout 31 March.

27 By the end of the battle in May these 'Rats of the Nam-Youm' numbered as many as three or four thousand – possibly the equivalent of up to five battalions – and (their lack of motivation or fighting qualities notwithstanding) the progressive removal of these men from the front line was another important factor in the eventual defeat of the French garrison. In a situation that was quite bizarre, this community carried on a thriving black market by recovering parachuted matériel and stealing equipment, which resulted in the units that were fighting being forced pragmatically to deal with those men who had opted out of the battle. Although the commanders were certainly tempted to do so, no attempt was made to attack and clear

out these deserters, for fear of precipitating an internecine war within the base. In any case, the nearby French units by various means ensured that these people could not escape from their self-imposed prison area, other than by re-joining the fighting units.

28 By the end of the fighting on 5 April, of the ten M-24 tanks of 3/1 RCC that had begun the battle in mid-March, there were just four serviceable tanks left at the main position, and two more still operational at Isabelle.

## Chapter 9

29 The position at Wieme had originally been designated 'Isabelle 5', but soon adopted the name of its commander. It was garrisoned by 219 T'ai tribesmen of Mobile Auxiliary Companies No. 431 and No. 432. Wieme was devoid of cover, defence stores, wire or (virtually) any mines. As a consequence of the high water table, its unrevetted trenches were no more than four feet deep and their bottoms were filled with mud. Wieme could only be reached from Isabelle's main position via a small bridge that was always under communist fire. Notwithstanding its uniquely inappropriate defensive arrangements, and despite a number of attempts by the Viet Minh to overrun it, strong-point Wieme held out until the fall of the main Isabelle position on the night of 7/8 May.

30 Colonel André Lalande was born on 26 May 1913. He attended St-Cyr in 1931 and was subsequently assigned to the 146e Régiment d'Infanterie de Fortresse at Metz. In May 1937 he was posted to the 6e Bataillon de Chasseurs Alpins at Grenoble. As a captain, he took part in the Narvik expedition in 1940, where he was seriously wounded. Once recovered (in England), he continued to serve with the Free French forces, joining 13 DBLE in Palestine on 1 January 1942. Subsequently, he fought at Halfaya Pass, Bir Hakeim, El Alamein and in Tunisia. Later, he served in Italy and France, taking command of 3/13 DBLE on 1 November 1944. Lalande was promoted lieutenant colonel on 25 March 1946, and then served in staff appointments until October 1953, when he volunteered for duty in Indo-China and assumed command of 3 REI. This appointment resulted in his deployment to Dien Bien Phu. He was captured on 8 May 1954 and repatriated on 4 September. Thereafter, he continued his military career, and eventually retired in 1973, with the rank of general.

## Chapter 10

31 However, twenty-four of the twenty-nine C-119 cargo aircraft that supplied Dien Bien Phu were flown by American civilian pilots who were contracted to the Taiwan-based Civil Air Transport Corporation (CAT). A small number of these pilots were in fact US military personnel, who had been seconded to the CAT mission in anticipation of the possible future direct involvement of the US in the war in Indo-China.

32 This assessment was made by General John W. O'Daniel, commanding US Army Pacific region, following a visit to Indo-China in June 1953.

33 Dulles was apparently much in favour of Operation 'Vulture'. This is interesting, given his lack of support for the strategically much more worthy Anglo-

French Suez operation in 1956. But from Washington's standpoint, the war in Indo-China was all about combating the common threat of communism, whereas Suez was viewed by many in the US administration as an Anglo-French attempt to perpetuate the pre-war European empires – which was anathema to the post-1945 US leadership.

34 The eight senior congressmen who attended this top secret meeting also stipulated that the French must continue to wage the war against the Viet Minh following any US intervention, while at the same time advancing their various Indo-Chinese territories rapidly to full independence – in order that the US would not be seen to have perpetuated a colonial regime.

35 See also Geraghty, pp. 247–9.

36 Many of the Operation 'Condor' troops firmly believed that they could have achieved much more to assist Dien Bien Phu. Soon afterwards, sixty-seven men deserted from 4 BCL, together with more than 25 per cent of 1 BPL.

## Chapter 11

37 The battle was fought during Napoleon III's ill-fated attempt to promote Archduke Maximilian as emperor of Mexico. At the village of Camerone, three officers and sixty-two other ranks of the 3rd Company, 1st Battalion of the Foreign Legion Regiment inflicted more than 300 casualties on an attacking force of infantry and cavalry that numbered almost 2,000. Two Legion officers and twenty-two other ranks were killed; one officer and eight other ranks died of their wounds soon after the battle; nineteen other ranks subsequently died in captivity; and one man, although wounded, evaded capture. Twelve other ranks from among those that were captured survived, and were eventually exchanged by the Mexicans. Subsequently, the wooden hand that the French commander, Captain Jean Danjou, had used since his own left hand was blown off in the Crimean War, was recovered from the battlefield and quickly became a revered relic of the Legion. Thereafter, the hand was paraded and duly honoured by the Legion on Camerone Day each year.

38 The theoretical (as recorded in French Army documents) cumulative strength of the garrison (casualties not taken into account) since 21 November 1953 stood at 16,544, plus 1,916 French and T'ai troops from Lai Chau (Operation 'Pollux') and 2,440 Viet Minh prisoners who had been airlifted to Dien Bien Phu to provide a pool of labour. The same source indicated French Union garrison casualties of 6,928 wounded and 1,293 dead from 21 November 1953 to 5 May 1954, although no official records exist for the garrison's casualties during the final three days of the conflict. See Fall's, *Hell in a Very Small Place*, pp. 431–2.

## Chapter 12

39 All accounts of the battle agree on the 1730 hours cease-fire time, but in his verbal orders to each commander de Castries' chief of staff, Lieutenant Colonel Séguin-Pazzis, is quoted as saying that the cease-fire would 'be effective as of 1700 hours'. This apparent discrepancy may be explained by the fact

that at the same time he ordered all remaining combat *matériel* to be destroyed, which action clearly could not be carried out after the end of hostilities but could presumably be done between 1700 and 1730 hours without attracting accusations of a breach of faith on the French part. He also reiterated formally that no white flags were to be displayed by the French troops at any time. But at least one account states that a white flag did indeed fly over de Castries' bunker for a short period of time prior to the arrival of the Viet Minh soldiers on 7 May, ostensibly 'to protect the wounded', but that it was quickly removed on Cogny's orders once the general in Hanoi became aware of its existence (see Roy, pp. 282–3).

40 De Castries' words certainly matched the character of the man, but the intention to 'fight to the end' (rather than meaning 'fighting on to the last man') undoubtedly meant that there would be no premature capitulation, and that the defence would continue until 1730 under French control and as planned. For some time, and even in the final minutes of the existence of the garrison of Dien Bien Phu, the French Union senior commanders were very aware that every word they had used – all of which had been meticulously recorded – would subsequently have considerable political implications, both for France and for them personally.

41 Despite the 1730 hours cease-fire time, the very last radio transmission made by the French Union garrison at Dien Bien Phu in fact came some twenty minutes later, at 1750 hours, when an unnamed French combat engineer radio operator somewhere in the area reported 'We're blowing up everything. *Adieu.*'

42 Ultimately, only the platoon of tank crewmen of 3/1 RCC maintained their cohesion and escaped the valley as a formed unit. Although it sustained casualties en route, six men of the platoon finally reached Muong Sai at the end of May, having negotiated 160 kilometres of enemy-held territory.

43 Apart from those would-be escapees killed subsequent to the fall of Isabelle, no more French Union soldiers died in combat at Dien Bien Phu after the end of the fight at Pom-Lot. The last French casualties as a direct result of the battle were probably the crewmen of a French naval Privateer bomber aircraft of Squadron No. 28-F which was shot down by Viet Minh anti-aircraft gunners towards the end of the night of 7/8 May, while bombing the communist lines of communication along Route 41, close to the valley. The nine aircrew were all killed.

**Chapter 13**

44 Final estimates for French Union casualties in the garrison at Dien Bien Phu from 21 November 1953 to 8 May 1954 vary – sometimes quite significantly – between accounts. Fall settles for final totals (including his estimates of casualties for the last three days) of about 2,093 dead and at least 7,728 wounded; Newman quotes 2,293 dead and 5,114 wounded; Watson and O'Neill arrive at figures of 2,293 dead and 5,134 wounded. Others quote varying figures that broadly match or fall within the spread of totals given in these sources. In any event, it is assessed that significantly more than 2,000 members of the French Union garrison died at

Dien Bien Phu, with more than 5,000 wounded; although the total number of casualties of all types incurred by all those personnel who were at various times situated within the garrison from 21 November 1953 to 8 May 1954 may very well have been as high as 9,000.

45 As had been the case during the battle, the Viet Minh concentrated their communist propaganda on the target audiences that they judged would be susceptible. Many of the Algerian soldiers, their homeland then on the brink of their own war for independence from France, plus some other groups and individuals, did succumb to what became categorised as 'brainwashing' following the political processing of US prisoners by the North Koreans and communist Chinese during the Korean War.

46 See also Fischer, *Les Camps*, pp. 38–40, and Fall's, *Hell in a Very Small Place*, pp. 437–8.

47 Fall, *Street Without Joy*, p. 31.

48 See also Geraghty, p. 242.

49 See Fall, *Street Without Joy*, p. 319. Viet Minh strengths were assessed to within 10 per cent accuracy, but their capabilities were not, and the relative capabilities of the French forces were consistently over-estimated.

50 On 7 March 1954 Giap also inflicted an important blow against the air support upon which the garrison of Dien Bien Phu depended, when a force of Viet Minh regular troops from People's Army Battalion No. 204, led by its deputy commander, Captain Minh Khanh, infiltrated Cot-Bi military airfield close to Haiphong and destroyed four B-26 bombers and six reconnaissance aircraft on the ground. This Viet Minh operation into the very heart of French-controlled territory shortly preceded the start of the main communist offensive at Dien Bien Phu.

51 The Geneva Agreement ended the French presence in Indo-China and also set the stage for the impending US involvement in Vietnam The Agreement established a cease-fire line along the 17th Parallel, and a 300 days period during which free movement was to take place across what subsequently became the border and de-militarised zone. The Viet Minh forces still in Laos and Cambodia were required to leave those countries. Finally, free elections to re-unite North and South Vietnam were scheduled for 1956. Given the clear ideological split between North and South Vietnam, underlined by the movement of some 900,000 civilians to the South and almost 100,000 Viet Minh and communist supporters and sympathisers to the North during the free movement period, the prospect of an early re-unification was somewhat optimistic. Meanwhile, some 1,000 Viet Minh soldiers remained in South Vietnam, in flagrant contravention of the Geneva Agreement; and held themselves in readiness for what was to become America's Vietnam War. {\rtf0\mac \deff0 {\fonttbl {\f0\froman Times;}

# INDEX

Entries for French Union military
units and strongpoints are selective.